PRAISE

GOD IS

In his book, *God Is Good*, Bill Johnson helps us understand profound faith that comes from Heaven and from the process of surrendering our will for His. We can only receive this from time spent in the Presence, "buying" oil with our time in the secret place like the Matthew 25 wise virgins.

I believe the words of this book will create in you a deeper hunger for God to transform your mind and your life. You are invited to become worshippers like David and Moses who wanted the Presence above all else. Bill is one of my dearest friends and heroes in the faith. As you read this thought-provoking book, it will take you to deeper levels of holy abandonment to the One you love!

HEIDI G. BAKER, PhD
Cofounder and CEO of Iris Global
Bestselling author of *Birthing the Miraculous*

As a Church, many of us have grown accustomed to hearing and saying, "God is good, all the time." But, how many of us actually believe this powerful statement? Bill Johnson's book, *God Is Good*, is surprisingly controversial, as it challenges hidden disbelief in the goodness of God and reminds us that there is infinitely more to be hopeful about, as our *true* hope is rooted and grounded in God's *true* character, which is perfectly and completely revealed in Jesus. I can think of no one more qualified than my good friend, Bill Johnson, to write about the goodness of God, as Bill quintessentially lives from the place of God's goodness. As a result, Bill manages to redefine our definitions and challenge us, the Body of Christ, to move beyond being convinced that God is good and instead make His goodness the air that we breathe, so that we may be fully enabled to "re-present" Jesus to a world in dire need of understanding and revelation about their Father.

DR. CHÉ AHN
Founding Pastor, HROCK Church, Pasadena, California
President, Harvest International Ministry
International Chancellor, Wagner Leadership Institute

It is my heartfelt desire and prayer that this incredible book would become a Christian classic. *God Is Good* is one of the most profoundly theologically sound books I have ever read on the goodness of our beloved Father God.

So many in the Church today have been tossed to and fro in the storms of life without a strong anchor, losing the hope set before them, embracing the enemies' lies about our Father's character and becoming weakened and double minded in their faith. And the root of it all has been the subtle defacing of our Father's character, by the enemy of our souls, the father of lies, with one intent—to confuse our battle lines; to weaken our souls, to rob, steal; and destroy the anchor of our hope which lies at the core of the foundation of our faith—the *goodness* of God.

If this core theological tenet is removed from our hearts, the Church will become weakened, paralyzed, and hopeless—a shadow of our incredible compassionate Father's intent for us. Bill Johnson is not only one of the most balanced, sound, and mature teachers in the Body of Christ today but also one of the most loved and most loving men I have ever encountered. Truly, he lives what he has written within these pages.

And so, I believe with *all* my heart that literally streams of living water will flow out of these pages as an impartation directly into your heart causing supernatural encounter, visitation, and revelation that will transform lives across the entire world.

That thousands upon thousands will dry their tears, rise up to battle with renewed hope and strength with a cry of gratitude to our beloved heavenly Father.

Thank you, thank you, thank you our beloved Bill Johnson for your courage in writing this profound book.

Let this cry ring out from churches all across the nations and resound in the spirit realm—*God Is Good!*

WENDY ALEC
Founder GOD TV
Bestselling author of *Visions from Heaven*

In his new book, *God Is Good*, Bill Johnson in his wonderful winsome way reveals how God, being a perfect Father, unfolds His fantastic plan. Being both perfect Love and perfect Truth uncompromised, He rescues us, redeems us, includes us, and commissions us to bring His Kingdom victoriously to the nations. The Old Testament Scriptures are wonderfully fulfilled by the New Testament. The revelations, teachings, lifestyle, and miracles of Jesus now become our model to see the Good News of the Kingdom transform, our world.

JOHN ARNOTT
Founder, Catch the Fire Toronto

It is a joy for me to recommend the latest book by my friend Bill Johnson. This book, *God Is Good*, unpacks the timely declaration about the nature and unchanging character of our Father who abounds in goodness. Walking close to the Lord and moving in His power and releasing His goodness involves more than simply having a right belief system of truths that are traditionally taught in the Church. What you believe about God's nature is destiny-defining. A.W. Tozer was absolutely correct—what we think and believe about God is absolutely essential.

To pray effectively, we need to be deeply rooted in the truth that God is good. There is more to this truth than one who only casually considers it might initially think. To believe for the miraculous and persevere for breakthrough, the central issue of God's goodness must be settled in our hearts and minds.

Bill Johnson is one of the most important voices in this generation. I love his books and have been helped and inspired by them. Many recognize Bill as a man who is an excellent and practical Bible teacher and one who operates in supernatural ministry. This is certainly true. At the same time, I respect and appreciate Bill because of his humility, kindness, and deep hunger for Jesus.

Bill is not afraid to address truths that are often held in tension in the Scripture, such as the sovereignty of God, the fear of the Lord, man's responsibility, or God's love and mercy. He doesn't overlook these key truths—*God Is Good* addresses these topics head-on. Bill has a passion to put truths in their appropriate context by emphasizing that *the Lord is good!* This is a much needed emphasis in the Church today.

Don't expect this book to answer every question you have. Bill doesn't attempt to do that. Yet, he equips us to answer the most important question of all: *Is God truly good?* When this truth is firmly established in our hearts, though our other questions will still exist—they simply won't weigh heavy on us, because we have come face to face with a most glorious and important truth: *God is good.* This one truth will change many things in the lives of sincere believers!

Get ready—I believe the Holy Spirit will use this book to lead you in a deeper encounter with our glorious God as He shows you how to practically live your everyday life in the light of His goodness.

MIKE BICKLE
Director, International House of Prayer of Kansas City
Bestselling author of *Passion for Jesus* and *Growing in Prayer*

Bill Johnson's latest book is the most important contemporary book I have read in our day. It perfectly captures the essence of creating a right view of God's very nature, and because of that it begins to address the theological battle that is happening right now in the church at large. He holds no punches in clarifying and even debunking some wrong understandings that the church has held in regard to judgment, law, and God's goodness among other incredible themes. I put the book down and just felt healthier and energized. I felt like I could articulate my faith in a new way, an empowered way. Bill basically is arming us with the weapons we need to fight the good fight of love. Like C.S. Lewis, Tozer, and other great modern Christian writers and thinkers, Bill has added a classic to be devoured.

SHAWN BOLZ
Author of *Translating God* and *Keys to Heaven's Economy*
www.bolzministries.com

Faith and love are like a magnifying glass. We hold a glass up to the sun and focus its rays on one tiny spot, and there is intense heat. Bill Johnson's book *God Is Good* has such incandescent focus. By faith and love, he emphasizes the Sun of Righteousness risen with healing in His wings (or beams).

I highly recommend this wonderful book!

EVANGELIST REINHARD BONNKE
Founder, Christ for All Nations
Author of *Evangelism by Fire* and *Taking Action*

At a crucial and dark season in the life of the nation of Israel, under the leadership of Moses in the wilderness, Moses interceded for the Children of Israel to be spared a much deserved judgment for apostasy. His entreaty of God is profound and moving in the Exodus 33 account. At a strategic moment in prayer, Moses then asks to behold God's glory. Mind you, Moses has seen manifestations of the glory already, yet in the heart of Moses, he yearned for something his spirit knew exceeded what he had seen and experienced already. Amazingly, God, in granting Moses' request, responds by saying: "I will make all my goodness pass before you and will proclaim before you my name 'The Lord.' And I will be gracious to whom I will be gracious, and will show mercy on whom I will show mercy." God's ultimate expression of His glory is His goodness! I hold deep admiration and respect for Pastor Bill Johnson. I not only count him a dear friend, I consider him one of the patriarchs in our generation in relation to the fullness of the Spirit and the heart of the Father. I know of no other voice that can take us on a journey into the very heart and nature of our "Good, Good Father" except Bill. The book you hold in your hand is not only a must have and a must read, it is a must read again and again. Absorb the profound insights regarding the nature of the Father and the Son, the reality of their intention to reveal their goodness to us by the power of the Holy Spirit, and the all too often overlooked theological compromising that takes place regarding the true nature of evil and the evil one that continues to find its way into our belief systems because of poor critical thinking skills when it comes to rightly diving the word of truth. Thanks, Bill, for your voice, your wisdom, your faithfulness to the truth, and your love for both God and His children.

Dr. Mark J. Chironna
Mark Chironna Ministries
Church on the Living Edge
Orlando, Florida

I have probably heard Bill Johnson speak about 100 times, but because these occasions were usually at conferences, I didn't get to hear the more nuanced understanding of some of Bill's teachings. I was so appreciative of the opportunity to read *God Is Good*. In this context, Bill was able to fully develop his teachings and to nuance them in a way that conferences do not allow. I loved *God Is Good*. It is a timely book, addressing hermeneutical issues of how to relate Old Testament and New Testament themes that seem to contradict until they are properly understood in context of the larger picture of the purposes of God.

While this book addresses theological issues, Bill deals with them in a very user-friendly manner, revealing how what one believes about God (one's theology) impacts everyday life. Topics include the freedom of the human will and the sovereignty of God; is God in control of all things, or is He directing things? Is God the author of sickness? How are we to understand the will of God? How are we to understand the authority of the believer? How do we explain the disappointment that comes when what we believe and what we experience aren't in agreement? What is the proper perspective on the nature of Jesus—did He work His miracles from His deity or in His humanity? What is the relationship between the goodness of God and the discipline of God, and many other theological concerns. I repeat, *God Is Good* is a timely book. In fact, there should be a recipe in the back giving directions on how to make barbecue out of *sacred cow* beef.

Well written, allowing the layperson to digest some important meat of theological debate. Overall, I felt the book was well balanced and dealt with many contemporary issues of theology in the twenty-first century. While deeply rooted in grace, it avoids the mistakes of the current hyper-grace teachings. Every pastor, Sunday school teacher, and leader in church should read *God Is Good*. This is vintage Bill Johnson. I had to resist the temptation to quote a few of the many one liners that are such profound statements. Way to go, Bill.

RANDY CLARK, D. MIN., THD
Overseer of the Apostolic Network of Global Awakening
Founder, Global Awakening
Bestselling author of *There Is More!*
and coauthor of *Essential Guide to Healing*

This is a really important book. The world is struggling to believe God is good; the Church is struggling, too. Bill invites us to rethink and reimagine what the Scriptures teach about how good God truly is. If we had the confidence Jesus had in His Father's goodness, we would be different people, and the world would be a different place. This book will challenge you, but the invitation toward a higher view of God is worth it!

JOHN ELDREDGE
Ransomed Heart Ministries
Bestselling author of *Wild at Heart, EPIC, Fathered by God,*
and *Moving Mountains*

I've often said that Bethel Church is the closest place to Heaven on earth. I think there is a reason for it and it's the theology held in this book about how good and how kind God is. God loves to manifest His presence when His essential nature of love and goodness is proclaimed. Bill Johnson has created a culture around this message that is affecting the globe. It shatters paradigms of religion that lock God's people up in unbelief and fear. This book is what I've needed as I'm still growing in the knowledge of how kind and good God is. Let's be transformed together as we read it.

Lou Engle
Founder of The Call
Author of *The Jesus Fast* and *Digging the Wells of Revival*

Absolutely paradigm-shifting. I cannot think of a more important book for our generation, providing answers to the Church's most critical and divisive questions. Within each page, you will be more and more convinced that God really is as good as you hoped He could be. A must-read for anyone who longs for deeper intimacy and relationship with their always-good Father.

Christa Black Gifford
Songwriter, speaker, author of *God Loves Ugly* and *Heart Made Whole*

With every historic movement of the Holy Spirit, a truth becomes illuminated concerning the nature of God. Five hundred years ago the Great Reformation was spearheaded by Martin Luther. A fire was lit when the Holy Spirit highlighted a verse in the Book of Romans: "The just shall live by faith." Progressive revelation came tumbling forth and church history was altered. In the past twenty years, another aspect of the nature of God is being highlighted by the Holy Spirit once again. This time it centers around the goodness of God. I have heard my friend Bill Johnson often say, "The best kept secret in the Body of Christ is that God is in a good mood!" I know no one better to adequately and appropriately address this subject today than Bill Johnson, as he and his team have created a contagious church culture at Bethel Church in Redding, California. All that they do, all the healing and miracles they see, is based in this one revelation concerning the nature of God. This book will be used to catapult this present move of God to new heights, widths, and depths. Thank you, Bill, for being such a good steward of the truth that *God Is Good!*

JAMES W. GOLL
Founder of God Encounters, Life Language Trainer, and CEO of GOLL Ideation LLC
Bestselling author of *The Seer, Lifestyle of a Prophet,* and *Dream Language*

I recommend Bill Johnson's book about God because I know Bill, I know his values, I know his stability as a teacher of the Word of God, and I know his gifted ministry. He is touching multitudes whose search has omitted the Bible, and that is the book out of which Bill speaks and points the way to the character, love, and power of the living God. Bill ministers God's Word, but he also leads people to experience God as Christ would do.

DR. JACK W. HAYFORD
Chancellor-Founder, The King's University, Southlake, Texas
Pastor Emeritus, The Church on the Way, Van Nuys, California

Transforming the world around us with the influence of Heaven is an impossible task apart from knowing the goodness of God. This revelation comes by dwelling in His presence. *God Is Good* by Bill Johnson is an invitation to discover the depths of God's heart and the greatness of His love for us. We may not always be able to comprehend the magnitude of His goodness, but that does not mean we can't experience the fullness of His goodness. *God Is Good* will help to tether you to His nature in such a way that through your encounter the world will experience His goodness leading to repentance and a redefinition of their relationship with Him.

LEIF HETLAND
Founder and President, Global Mission Awareness
Bestselling author of *Seeing Through Heaven's Eyes*

There are some books you read and you feel uplifted. Reading other books challenges your faith to grow.

However, unlike any of those, Bill Johnson's book, *God Is Good*, has left an indelible mark upon my soul. Portions of my thinking needed to be nudged back into alignment. My theology was straight, but my heart needed a fresh reminder of the One I love.

Please read this book. You will have a seal of love set upon your heart too.

CINDY JACOBS
Cofounder of Generals International
Bestselling author of *Possessing the Gates of the Enemy*

This book reveals both deep compassion and a passion for revival reflecting God's heart. Bill Johnson emphasizes how we must hear and embrace God's heart in Scripture. God really is good and does want what is best for us. Although in this fallen world God uses suffering and often calls us into it, God's original and ideal, kind purpose for us is evident in the perfect, promised Kingdom. Blessings God provides us in this world, including healings and spiritual gifts, are marvelous foretastes of that Kingdom.

DR. CRAIG KEENER
Professor of Biblical Studies, Asbury Theological Seminary
Author of *Acts: An Exegetical Commentary* and *Miracles: The Credibility of New Testament Accounts*

Bill Johnson is one of the most unusual men of our generation. God has used him to bless countless people from all over the world. I regard Bill as my friend. Agree or disagree with him at certain points, here is a man who loves Jesus with all his heart and deserves to be heard. I hope this book will be a blessing to you.

R.T. KENDALL
Minister of Westminster Chapel (1977-2002)
Bestselling author of *Total Forgiveness*

Over the course of many years, I have sat under countless life-giving, revelatory messages and teachings about God and His glorious Kingdom through Pastor Bill Johnson. Each one has profoundly impacted and satiated my hungry soul. I love his new book, *God Is Good*, because the revealing of the goodness of God is one of the most vital and life-giving foundational threads of truth found in all his sermons and previous books.

How wonderful to discover all those beautiful strands of revelation skillfully collected into one book. *God Is Good* will transform and establish you in the truth regarding God's heart for you, His church, and the world. I want to read this book over and over again. You will too!

Patricia King
Patricia King Ministries
Author of *Spiritual Revolution* and *Decree*
www.patriciaking.com

On rare occasions a message comes along that is so life-giving and life-changing we can never see ourselves, the Word, or the world the same after encountering it. Bill Johnson's new book, *God Is Good*, is one of those messages. Every paragraph is a word of wisdom. Lightning bolts of revelation strike on every page. I found myself stopping often to reflect on one profound insight after another. I can't wait to read it again. I highly recommend *God Is Good* for your personal reading as well as your family, church, and study group.

Daniel Kolenda
President and CEO, *Christ for All Nations*
Author of *Live Before You Die*

This is the book that I have been waiting for. There is not a more important yet more misunderstood topic than our view of God's goodness. It is the foundation we are to establish our lives on. The very nature of God's goodness is what draws people to Jesus. The goodness of God is better than we could ever think or imagine. I am eternally grateful to Bill Johnson for laying that foundation in my own walk with the Lord. How we see God affects every area of our lives. In *God Is Good*, Bill clearly lays out the biblical basis for the goodness of God and answers the very tough questions that trip us up when wrestling with this subject. This book will challenge you in the best way possible and awaken your heart to the depths of His goodness. I am so, so happy you've picked this book up because of the life-changing revelation you're about to encounter.

BANNING LIEBSCHER
Founder and Pastor of Jesus Culture
Author of *Jesus Culture* and *Rooted*

Bill Johnson's new book, *God Is Good*, reminds us again that despite all the evil in the world, God is true to His essential character—He is good. I recommend this book to everyone who has any questions about the wonderful goodness of our God.

DR. VINSON SYNAN
Dean Emeritus, Regent University School of Divinity
Author of *Century of the Holy Spirit*

It is an honor and a privilege for me to write an endorsement for Apostle Bill Johnson. Being the man of God he is, I am honored to know him personally and by the Spirit. He is one of the greatest and most powerful apostles of the end times—and I do not say that lightly.

Apostle Bill Johnson has trained, equipped, and activated thousands of people around the world to move in the supernatural power of God. He continues to teach multitudes how to bring Heaven to earth—making Heaven real—to invade the impossibilities people face in their life and ministry. He is a father and an example in the Spirit to this generation.

Many people write good books yet lack revelation because they have not experienced what they are writing about. However, this new book, *God Is Good*, is certainly full of powerful and transforming revelation for two reasons—Apostle Bill Johnson has had an experience with the goodness of God and he knows Him. Because he writes from those two places, this book will activate countless people to have a personal encounter with the goodness and power of God.

As you read *God Is Good*, you will learn how to bring heaven on earth, to be activated to walk in the supernatural and to be a carrier of the presence of God, and will be led to have an encounter with the Holy Spirit. I greatly recommend this book! It will have an enormous impact on your life.

APOSTLE GUILLERMO MALDONADO
Senior leader of King Jesus International Ministry, Miami, Florida
Bestselling author of *The Glory of God* and *The Kingdom of Power*

Bill Johnson stands tall among the great spiritual leaders of the world. Bethel Church in Redding, California, is the scene of the clearest expression of genuine revival to be found on the planet. This book is supremely relevant on a vital topic and challenges all of us to display the goodness of God. A must read! Thanks, Bill!

JACK TAYLOR
President of Dimensions Ministries

I just love Bill Johnson's book, *God Is Good*. He shows the inconsistency of our theology as we believe God sends sickness to teach us, and yet we go to the doctor attempting to alleviate the sickness. He persuasively maintains that theology must be wrapped in experience and must be congruent with the lifestyle of Jesus, who was perfect theology.

Bill declares it is time to quit celebrating when darkness envelops the earth and instead be a beacon on the hilltops, shining God's glory upon our cities. It is time for the Church to be the head and not the tail, to command, "Thy Kingdom come," to heal the sick, to cast out demons, to be the light of the world. I say, "Amen!"

DR. MARK VIRKLER
President of Christian Leadership University
Bestselling author of *4 Keys to Hearing God's Voice*

Wow! Right from the start, this book tackles the nature of God's goodness by exposing the lies that disable believers from fully trusting our Father. Be ready to be astounded with another great masterpiece full of simple yet challenging revelations that will help to strengthen the very foundation of our faith! I can personally attribute the very core of my belief system and faith walk to listening to what Bill has said and applying those principles daily. I recommend this book to every believer and self-proclaimed atheists. Outstanding!

TODD WHITE
Lifestyle Christianity

God is good—He certainly is! The pages of this book are filled with revelation after revelation of the goodness of God. Whatever season you are walking through, God's nature toward us is unchanging. I am confident that as you invite the Holy Spirit to reveal this truth to your heart of hearts, your life will truly never be the same.

DARLENE ZSCHECH
Internationally recognized worship leader
Songwriter of "Shout to the Lord," "The Potter's Hand"
and "The Victor's Crown"

The writer of Hebrews says, the Son is "the exact representation of His [the Father's nature]" and John says, "He has explained Him." And yet, when someone called Jesus good, He responded that no one is good, but God!

Bill Johnson's grasp of the whole of Scripture confronts the broad spectrum of specious reasonings that militate against this fundamental truth that are fulfilling Jeremiah's ancient indictment. "For My people have committed two evils: They have forsaken Me, the fountain of living waters, And hewn themselves cisterns—broken cisterns that can hold no water."

BISHOP JOSEPH L. GARLINGTON, SR.
Pastor of Covenant Church of Pittsburgh
Author of *Worship* and *Right or Reconciled*

GOD
is
GOOD

DESTINY IMAGE BOOKS BY BILL JOHNSON

Hosting the Presence

Hosting the Presence Every Day

When Heaven Invades Earth

The Supernatural Power of the Transformed Mind

Strengthen Yourself in the Lord

Releasing the Spirit of Prophecy

Dreaming with God

Here Comes Heaven

Release the Power of Jesus

The Supernatural Ways of Royalty

Spiritual Java

A Life of Miracles

Center of the Universe

Dream Journal

A Daily Invitation to Friendship with God

GOD
—— is ——
GOOD

HE'S BETTER
THAN YOU THINK

BILL
JOHNSON

DESTINY IMAGE® PUBLISHERS, INC.

P.O. Box 310, Shippensburg, PA 17257-0310

"Promoting Inspired Lives."

This book and all other Destiny Image and Destiny Image Fiction books are available at Christian bookstores and distributors worldwide.

Cover design by Christian Rafetto

Interior design by Terry Clifton

For more information on foreign distributors, call 717-532-3040.

Reach us on the Internet: www.destinyimage.com.

ISBN 13 HC: 978-0-7684-3716-4

ISBN 13 eBook: 978-0-7684-1836-1

ISBN 13 978-0-7684-1742-5

For Worldwide Distribution, Printed in the U.S.A.

1 2 3 4 5 6 7 8 / 22 21 20 19 18

I dedicate this book to Beni, my wife of 43 years. "You are a daily reminder to me of God's goodness. Your love for God, me, our family, and life in general is inspirational. Experiencing your love and sharing your life is one of the ways I am able to 'taste and see that the Lord is good.' I love you."

—Bill

ACKNOWLEDGMENTS

I thank Michael Van Tinteren and Kristy Tillman, my assistants, for their assistance with scheduling and research. I am especially grateful to Pam Spinosi for her help in editing my material—priceless work. Much thanks to Dann Farrelly and the BSSM team for their amazing job on the Addendum. Also, much thanks to Larry Sparks of Destiny Image for his encouragement and patience in the "longer-than-normal writing process" needed for *God Is Good*. You all represent Him well. Thanks.

CONTENTS

FOREWORD

The statement "God is good" is so much more than a catchy Christian slogan. It's more than a theological statement. The love of God, the nature of God, and the character of God are all completely and entirely *good*. He can't be anything else.

What you believe about God's goodness impacts every aspect of your life. In the same way, how you pray is determined by who you think God is. Does He want to answer your prayer? Does He still heal today? Does He still set the captives free? Does He still move mountains and reverse impossible situations?

In this landmark book, Bill Johnson has done something that, I believe, will help Christ-followers better understand who God is, and, in turn, applying this knowledge will connect them to their destinies.

So, how does knowing God is good have anything to do with fulfilling our destinies and callings in Christ?

As believers, we are destined to be ambassadors and representatives of Jesus. One of the great messages Bill brings to the Body of Christ is that we are empowered to *faithfully represent* Jesus through the power of the Holy Spirit. What Jesus did, we can do too. While others teach about representing Jesus, Bill's emphasis is often on *faithfully* representing Him.

Sadly, I have seen many people who claim to represent Jesus, but in actuality, they're misrepresenting Him. Some do it out of misguided religious zeal. Some do it purely out of ignorance; they mean well but are uninformed about *who* God really is. Others misrepresent Him out of heretical and dangerous theology. Whatever the reason, the fact remains: There are and will always be poor representations of Jesus in this world.

The truth is, we need to see Him differently so we can represent Him accurately. Jesus doesn't need to change anything; *we do.* He doesn't need to become "more" good; He already *is* good.

What the world needs is a prophetic voice who will call out to the Body of Christ and ask them to stand up and faithfully represent Jesus. I believe Bill does just that in this book. This book is a prophetic call to the Body of Christ from a man who deeply knows and interacts with the God he writes about. In a friendly, even fatherly tone, he helps guide you through Scripture—Old Testament to the New—on an eye-opening journey to discovery that will radically transform the way you see and interact with God.

Robert Morris
Founding Senior Pastor, Gateway Church
Bestselling Author of *The Blessed Life,*
The God I Never Knew, Truly Free, and *Frequency*

INTRODUCTION

The subject of God's goodness shouldn't be all that hard to write about. It's one of the most obvious realities in existence. Yet this book has been a challenge. If ever there were a temptation to wait until my understanding was more complete before taking on such a writing project, this would be the time.

I have more questions than answers. And I am certain that what I've written will bring many challenges to some, just as it will bring help to others. Yet I have one reason for writing it—God told me to do so. Really. He spoke to me during a pastor's prayer meeting, when I was not specifically thinking about writing—particularly, writing about the subject of God's goodness. We were sharing testimonies about God's wonderful work in our city, and as He so often does, He interrupted my thoughts with a very strong internal impression.

While it wasn't audible, it was close. "I want you to write about Me being good." I've never had that happen before with any of my books. I've brought ideas to Him and asked for confirmation, and I've sought Him for specific direction regarding a writing assignment, but I've never had Him give me a mandate like this. While I know many use "God told me to do it" as an excuse to do what they want, in this case, it is my story.

I offer this as an act of obedience, to the best of my ability. As you consider this priceless subject called God's goodness, I do pray you will join me in never sacrificing what you know about God to the questions that remain unanswered.

Enjoy.

—BILL

Chapter One

CONFLICT OVER GOODNESS

What comes into our minds when we think about
God is the most important thing about us.

—A.W. TOZER

The greatest shift of seasons in the history of planet Earth came with an announcement given by angels—*Peace and goodwill toward men!* (See Luke 2:14.) This plan had been in waiting since before the worlds were made, but it needed to be withheld until the right moment. Sin filled the earth, people were out of touch with God's perspective for their lives, and there was little passion to know the one true God throughout the world—the timing was perfect.

Most of us celebrate this message at Christmastime every year. This decree revealed God's heart more clearly than ever before. It redefined God's intent for humanity, which so far has lasted two thousand years. But after all these years, many of us have not shifted our thinking to be consistent with His announced plan—one of peace and goodwill. Without a shift in thinking, it will be all too easy to misrepresent this magnificent One by expecting and allowing things to take place *on our watch* that Jesus never would have allowed.

HE'S A FATHER

If I were to do to my children what many people think God does to His children, I'd be arrested for child abuse. People say God is good, yet they credit Him with causing cancer and natural disasters and even blame Him for terrorist activities. Some try to escape the pain of such shameful reasoning by stating, "He allowed it" instead of "He caused it." In my way of thinking, there's little to no difference. If I abuse my children, or "allow/approve" a neighbor to do it, it's obvious I have a very serious problem. And when we sweep the abusive misdeed under the carpet called *God works in mysterious ways,* we add insult to injury. There is a common thought among many that God causes or allows evil to take place so He can display His mercy. That would be like me breaking my child's arm to show my ability to give him comfort, and then using my skills to reset the broken bone. People ask me, "What about Job?" My response is, "What about Jesus?" Job provides the question. Jesus gives the answer. The story of Job is about holding to our faith in the midst of trials and seeing God restore everything brilliantly. But the story of Jesus is the only one I follow.

There's no question that God can turn any situation around for His glory and for our benefit—this of course includes the most evil

> **People ask me, "What about Job?" My response is, "What about Jesus?" Job provides the question. Jesus gives the answer.**

conditions known to humanity around the world. But that is the testimony of His greatness and His redemptive purpose. It does not represent His design. To attribute evil to Him tragically undermines our purpose on the earth, as it cripples our ability to *re*-present Jesus as the manifestation of God's *goodwill toward men*. Our boldness to declare and demonstrate who He is in a given situation is seriously impaired if we're not confident of what He is like. When the boldness that is normal to the one filled with the Spirit of God diminishes, it costs us dearly. It is often our boldness that draws Him into an impossible situation.

> *Now, Lord, look on their threats, and grant to Your servants that **with all boldness they may speak** Your word, by stretching out Your hand to heal, and that signs and wonders may be done through the name of Your holy Servant Jesus* (Acts 4:29–30).

What might be even more devastating in this view of God causing evil is that it ultimately compromises our ability to discern the difference between God's discipline and an actual demonic assault. And that is a weakness that we cannot afford to carry around any longer. People constantly embrace a hellish situation in their lives because of the thought that God intended it for good. That way of thinking infects the God-given ability to discern the works of the devil with a human reasoning that is demonic in nature. In fact, it's not just discernment that is in question. This kind of breakdown in our assignment to spiritual maturity causes us to forget who the enemy really is and what we're actually fighting against. Jesus gave us all we needed to know—*"The thief comes only to steal and kill and destroy; I came that they may have life, and have it abundantly. I am the good shepherd; the good shepherd lays down His life for the sheep"* (John 10:10–11). It's not complicated. Loss, death, and destruction are the things left behind when the devil has had influence in a given situation. Jesus is the *Good* Shepherd. And what does that goodness look like? He gives abundant life. Here it is—loss, death, and destruction vs. abundant life. One is bad; the other is good. It shouldn't be that hard to distinguish between the two. And if that wasn't enough, John summarized why Jesus came to earth: *"The Son of God appeared for this purpose, to destroy the works of the devil"* (1 John 3:8). Jesus taught us how to recognize the works of the devil and then modeled how we destroy them. Do we have the right to set a new way of life and ministry that doesn't do what Jesus commanded us to do? No. Absolutely not!

It is time to reexamine our belief system and find out what the Bible really teaches about the nature of God. It really comes down to this—many have rejected the clear revelation of the nature of God that is seen in the person of Jesus Christ.

IS GOD GOOD?

Almost every believer confesses that God is good. We have to. It's in the Bible. It's not the belief in His goodness that threatens us. It's our definition of this goodness that has brought much debate and sometimes conflict and turmoil into the family of God.

If He is as good as many claim, how we respond to this truth will require massive change in how we do life. Instead of creating doctrines that explain away our weakness and anemic faith, we'll actually have to find out why *"the greater works than these"* have not been happening in and around us (see John 14:12). Creating doctrines of *no miracles today* not only contradicts His Word, it is a sneaky way to avoid responsibility. Instead of changing the standard for life given by Jesus, who walked the earth two thousand years ago, we are to embrace it and follow His model. We were designed with the capacity to be conformed into the likeness of Jesus, the One who is resurrected from the dead and is seated at the right hand of the Father (see 1 John 4:17). We'll deal with that later. But the bottom line is, it was never meant that the hour we live in was to be inferior to Jesus' earthly ministry. It's quite the opposite.

> *Most assuredly, I say to you, he who believes in Me, the works that I do he will do also; and greater works than these he will do, because I go to My Father* (John 14:12).

The Pharisees saw Jesus as a threat to their positions of power and influence. In a similar way, many leaders today feel threatened over a possible shift in theological positions that implies we've not been as successful in ministry as we could have been. We empower the lie we believe. The fight to protect the sanctity of our history has kept us from a more significant future. I'm thankful for my past. I'm thankful for what our forefathers fought for, so that we might live in greater liberty in Christ. But there is more. And things are about to change because the greatest harvest of souls of all time is about to come in. And it won't come because of our advanced skills in preaching, our use of media, or even our powerful music. Each of those areas has importance, but they do not exist unto themselves. They are important in that they are vehicles that carry the greatest revelation of all time—God is good, and He is a perfect Father.

His goodness is beyond our ability to comprehend, but not our ability to experience. Our hearts will take us where our heads can't fit.

His goodness is beyond our ability to comprehend, but not our ability to experience. Our hearts will take us where our heads can't fit. Understanding is vital, but it often comes through experiencing God. Faith for the journey of walking with God leads to encounters with God. It results in a growing knowledge and understanding of truth, as in *"by faith we understand that the worlds were framed by the word of God"* (Heb. 11:3). Having said that, one of the great commands of Scripture pertaining to the experience of His goodness is *"taste and see that the Lord is good"* (Ps. 34:8). If you'll *taste it* for yourself, you'll *see it* more clearly. Your perception of truth will increase as you experience truth more deeply.

As it is with this most important doctrine of *being born again*, we always understand a subject more clearly once we've experienced it. Hearing someone teach on being born again who isn't born again is almost laughable. There is hardly a group of believers anywhere that would treasure that teaching. Yet a similar practice is almost applauded as noble in much of Christendom—theology that requires no experience. I realize that some may assume I mean that theology is based on experience, which implies to some we throw reason out the door. That is a true and present danger. But the issue that has had much more damage in present-day church life is theology without experience. The Pharisees were known for theories that never had an effect on their own lives. To combat this, we must exercise our faith to put a demand on what we believe. Simple mental assent must not be the end of the story.

COMMON BELIEFS MUST BE CHALLENGED!

Changing our theology doesn't change Him. Either He is authentically good, or He is not. I would never suggest that we pretend He is different than He is. Nothing is accomplished by allowing our imagination to create our own image of God. He would then be no better than the gods made out of wood or stone, also created by human initiative. Inventing Him in our minds or building Him with our hands is a similarity that is both vain and ultimately destructive. Discovering who He is and what He is like in reality is the only possible way to discover His true goodness. This eternal journey into His infinite goodness is the one we are privileged to embrace.

I've heard people say they don't believe in God anymore after experiencing a disappointment or tragic loss of some sort. I don't mean to treat their situation with disregard, but you can't turn a consciousness of God on and off like that. You may be mad at God. You may accuse Him and refuse to serve Him. But you can't decide He no longer exists. To claim atheism as a belief system doesn't get rid of Him. It merely deadens a person's awareness of Him and attempts to remove the awareness of his need for Him from the context of daily life. Merely changing our theology changes us, not Him. But when what we believe is anchored in the reality of who He is, earth comes into agreement with Heaven where the reality of His world increasingly invades ours, manifested in both power and glory.

It's impossible for us to create a concept of what He is like that is greater than He really is. He is either greater than we can understand, perceive, describe, or imagine, or He is not God—we are. Neither can we exaggerate His goodness. We can twist it, pervert it, dilute it, and misrepresent it. But the one thing we cannot do is exaggerate the goodness of God. It will take us all of eternity just to broach the subject of His goodness. The apostle Paul gives us an extremely challenging promise in this regard. Ephesians 3:20–21: *"Now to Him who is able to do far more abundantly beyond all that we ask or think, according to the power that works within us, to Him be the glory in the church and in Christ Jesus to all generations forever and ever. Amen."*

The phrase *"beyond all that we ask or think"* is quite impressive. *"Beyond all we ask"* addresses the impact of our prayers, which include both those that are outwardly expressed and the secret cries of the heart. What God does for us is beyond the reach of our biggest prayer on our greatest day with our highest level of faith—He exists in that realm to work for us. *"Beyond all we think"* is another very powerful statement dealing with the impact of our imagination. This describes us on our best day, with our most well-thought-out dreams, plans, goals, and imaginations. His commitment to us is to function beyond the limitations of our imagination and perform the unthinkable on our behalf. These are expressions of His goodness, which come from His being. He is perfect goodness personified.

I said "yes" to this journey many years ago and have since discovered that His goodness is beyond my wildest dreams. My *yes* started by simply recognizing that I have sinned and fallen short of God's purpose and design. Jesus then became for me the perfect manifestation of goodness. He rescued me from all that would destroy me and brought me into a relationship with Him where more of His goodness could be discovered. Many have taken that first step but tragically have stopped after step one, picking up the view of *who God is* as seen in the Old Testament stories. Those stories are important and necessary. But the fact is, Jesus came to replace them with a clearer view of what God is like. There are few deceptions more devastating than this one. It is tragic and so completely unnecessary.

CIVIL WAR IN THE CHURCH

The one thing that concerns me most in the day in which we live is the possibility of another civil war. The reality of that potential conflict is upon us right now. However, it's not racial, political, or economic. Neither is it fought between groups with differing moral or social agendas. While those tensions obviously exist in society, they have permission to exist because of the division that is celebrated in the Church. We set the stage. It's tough to get reconciliation in the factions that exist in the world around us when the Church itself sponsors the wars of internal conflict with religious delight.

I'm referring to a war within the family of God—it is spiritual. This one is not being fought with guns and bombs. It's being fought with words of accusation, character assassination, ridicule, and slander. The conflict is over the goodness of God. That spirit of accusation is welcomed in many circles as the voice of reason, the voice of discernment. My prayer is that through an arresting revival in the nations, we will see another Great Awakening that dismantles the tsunami of the demonic that thrives on our self-righteous theology and the corresponding division it creates.

We will know our mind is renewed when the impossible looks logical.

The Church isn't known for handling conflict well. We tend to be the only army in the world that shoots their wounded, especially if they were wounded through their own doing. When there are doctrinal conflicts, there are books written and radio shows broadcasted to expose and shame those attempting to serve God with their best effort to teach truth. Good theology is essential. But theology without love is a loud clanging cymbal—annoying at best. I believe that a true discovery of the goodness of God could heal this issue for us all.

THE HEAVENLY MIND

The biblical concept of the renewed mind is in part an answer to this problem. It is made available to us as a gift from a good Father— it is the mind of Christ. The renewed mind is more than having the ability to give a biblical answer to a problem. It includes that, but in reality, it is so much more. It is seeing from a divine perspective.

And do not be conformed to this world, but be transformed by the renewing of your mind, so that you may prove what the will of God is, that which is good and acceptable and perfect (Romans 12:2).

In the Romans passage, the renewed mind proves the will of God. That is fascinating when you realize that the best definition for the will of God in Scripture is *"Your will be done, on earth as it is in heaven"* (Matt. 6:10). It can be said that the renewed mind is what reveals and illustrates God's will on earth. The mind of Christ, seen in Jesus' lifestyle, illustrates this beautifully. He confronted storms, healed bodies, multiplied food, and did countless other miracles to reveal Heaven's effect on earth. The renewed mind in us should do the same. We will know our mind is renewed when the impossible looks logical.

Yet there's another twist provided in the word *prove*. It can also be translated "approve." Let me illustrate. If I were the world's greatest art specialist and authority on Vincent van Gogh paintings, and you discovered a painting signed "Vincent van Gogh" in an estate you inherited, you'd want my services to evaluate whether or not it's an authentic masterpiece. If it's real, it could be worth one hundred million dollars. If it's a fake, it may be worth one hundred dollars. My approval makes quite the difference in what someone would be willing to pay to purchase such a potential treasure. The burden of proof is then put upon my shoulders. If the painting is authentic, it will be celebrated worldwide as a great new discovery. If it's a fake, it must be labeled as such so no one is duped into buying something that has very little value.

My process of study would include the examination of every brushstroke of your painting to see if it's consistent with his style. I would also test the colors, paints, and canvas to see if they're similar to ones we know are consistent with his known works. It would also be prudent in my examination to research the subject of the painting to see if I could place the location or content with what we know about his life. If after weeks of examination, I put my approval on your piece of art as *a previously unknown Vincent van Gogh painting*, you, of course, would be ecstatic. The news of my authentication of your painting would hit the art world worldwide within minutes. You would then need to decide whether you wanted to keep the piece for your own enjoyment, display it in a museum for others to enjoy, or auction it to the highest bidder. Please note that such an approval is not a careless opinion, as my entire reputation as a specialist is at risk. It has to be a scholarly conclusion based on the study of previous works as well as the known nature and life of the artist himself.

Discovering the will of God in some of our most difficult situations is often as easy as using the same reasoning offered through this illustration. For example, if someone calls me on the phone and tells me that the sickness I am suffering from has been given to me by God to teach me to trust Him, I need to examine his word to see if it is an authentic word from God. God, the Chief of all artists, has left us with many masterpieces throughout Matthew, Mark, Luke, and John. The stories of the Master's touch abound as person after person is healed and delivered by the love of this perfect Father. As I study these four Gospels, I must take note that I can't find any "painting" with the same strokes or colors. There's not one example of Jesus giving a disease to anyone. In fact, His lifestyle was the opposite. What the person claims is an authentic word from God contradicts the examples of His known works. The renewed mind is able to come to the conclusion that what was given to me with God's signature at the bottom is in fact a forgery. The nature of this deceptive piece is so severe that it requires me to expose it as a fraud so that no one buys the counterfeit art in His name. And even though I soundly reject this person's word to me, I don't reject the person. I know that my approach to that person sets the standard for how I am to be treated in my day of need. *"Blessed are the merciful, for they shall receive mercy"* (Matt. 5:7). He is to be valued for who he is in God, not because he gets everything right. None of us do. In the Old Testament, the prophet was judged if he gave a wrong word. In the New Testament, the word is to be judged.

Tragically, many forgeries are accepted by believers day after day and then sold to others in the Christian marketplace as authentic revelations of the will of God. They in turn distort the revealed will of God throughout the Scriptures, perverting our sense of what He is like. The biggest forgery of all just might be the teaching that Jesus no longer heals people from sickness and delivers them from torment. Simple examination of Scripture proves that such a concept is a devilish misrepresentation of the One who gave Himself to reveal the Father and redeem humanity. Many good people believe such lies. They must be treated with kindness—they were poisoned with a lie. But it's equally true that the lies they promote must be exposed as forgeries. What causes me the most grief is that this way of thinking misrepresents the nature of God. It hurts our approach to life, seriously damaging our ability to represent Him as good. Perhaps it's these forgeries that have been marketed for decades by well-meaning believers that have contributed to the single greatest vacuum in human consciousness—the knowledge of the goodness of God.

LIKE CUTTING WOOD

A number of years ago, I heard a pastor tell us about a building project he once had for his church. He told us of how much he wanted to help the contractor in the building process. He was obviously excited for the new project, but because he had no building skills, it wasn't easy to find a place for him to fit in. He was persistent in asking if there was any work he could do. His enthusiasm over their building project finally persuaded the contractor to find something for him to do. The contractor told him that he needed one hundred two-by-fours cut to eight feet in length for the next morning. The pastor was excited that he got to be involved in his own church project. So after everyone else left for the night, the pastor stayed and cut the lumber. He took the first piece of wood, measured eight feet with his tape measure, and marked it. He then carefully cut it to eight feet exactly. Instead of using the tape measure for the second piece of wood to be cut, he used the previously cut board, as he thought that would be so much easier. He laid it on top of the new one, carefully drew a line where that board needed to be cut, and sawed off the part that was too long. He then took that newly cut board and placed it on top of the next piece that needed to be cut. He used this method of measuring throughout his assignment to cut one hundred boards.

I'm sure you can see the problem. By using the previously cut board as the measure, the next board is marked and cut about one-eighth of an inch too long. This process wouldn't have been so devastating had he only had two or three boards to cut. But when that method is used for one hundred boards, you end up with the ones at the end of the pile being over nine feet long.

For two thousand years, we've been comparing ourselves to the previous generation, noticing only slight differences. And to console ourselves with the task at hand—the Great Commission to disciple nations, displaying the greater works—many create watered-down doctrines that dismantle the example and commandments that Jesus gave us. Instead of comparing ourselves with ourselves, we should have been using the original standard found in the life of Jesus so that the measure of God's goodness revealed in Christ would have remained the same through the past two thousand years. God is bringing us back to the original measurement so that He might be revealed more accurately as the Father who loves well.

Chapter Two

IN THE BEGINNING

What I see in the Bible, especially in the book of Psalms, which is a book of gratitude for the created world, is a recognition that all good things on Earth are God's, every good gift is from above. They are good if we recognize where they came from and if we treat them the way the Designer intended them to be treated.

—PHILIP YANCEY

Because God is better than I think, I must adjust my thinking and the tenderness of my heart until I live conscious of both His nature and His presence. And that awareness then becomes the reality I live from. His nature defines who I am and what I do. This greatest reality of all realities is to become my spiritual, emotional, and intellectual home. In the same way, I travel from my home to my office, or from my home to minister in another country, so

His nature is to become the home I travel from—it is the reference point for all of life. And though I travel great distances from my home, I am never to be away from the awareness of His goodness. That is the home or the abiding place of my heart that goes with me everywhere.

He longs to reveal Himself to those who are ready to fully embrace what they discover. In many ways, our *yes* precedes seeing more of Him. Our *yes* is our invitation for more of Him. Revelation of truth releases responsibility for truth. Revelation is seldom given to those who are merely curious. You'll never see Him reveal truth just to make us smarter or more capable of debating with those who see differently. Truth by nature is the transforming power of God to instill freedom in the life of those who embrace it. It could be said that freedom exists in a person's life to the degree he embraces truth from the heart. It's more than a mental agreement to a concept called truth. It is the heartfelt *yes* to a way of life. That way of life becomes measureable in our lifestyle of freedom. Jesus put it this way: *"You will know the truth, and the truth will make you free"* (John 8:32). My journey starts to break down when my thoughts violate who He is. When our questions express our hunger for discovery, they're fruitful. But when our questions challenge who He is, they are foolish and lead to intellectual pride and ultimately spiritual barrenness.

Who He is is revealed in what He says. He identifies Himself as the Word. In other words, He says nothing apart from who He is. His Word reveals His nature and manifests His presence. Jesus was never a broadcaster of truths He didn't live. Even the people of His day recognized this as a reason for His unequalled authority—*"Never has a man spoken the way this man speaks"* (John 7:46).

Lies are costly, as they steal life from all who embrace them. Tragically, if I believe a lie, I empower the liar. The devil is the enemy of our souls. He works to trip us up through lies, intimidation, accusation, and seduction. His aim is to get us to question who God really is. His first interaction with Adam and Eve was to get them to question God's motives for giving a command not to eat the forbidden fruit, which was from the Tree of the Knowledge of Good and Evil. Satan said, *"You surely will not die! For God knows that in the day you eat from it your eyes will be opened, and you will be like God, knowing good and evil"* (Gen. 3:4–5). He accuses God of using His commands to protect Himself from humanity by keeping people from becoming like Him, knowing good and evil. Such nonsense was the tool used to poison humanity at its core.

This great deception released a curse into the human race. Tragically, Adam and Eve ate the forbidden fruit to become like God. They tried to obtain through an act what they already had by design—they were created in the image of God. They were already like Him! Willful disobedience will never bring us increase but will instead cause us to lose what little we have. Their disobedience made them like the one they obeyed—the serpent. For this reason, Jesus came as the Rescuer, crushing the serpent's head in the process. (See Genesis 3:15.)

Entertaining a lie still can have an effect on us—spirit, soul, and body. It's a poison that works into our being to destroy our identity and purpose. The devil lies about who God is and, in turn, who we are. It's all about identity. Through rebellion, satan lost his place of identity with God for eternity. He is trying to do the same to the only part of all creation that was made in God's image.

I can't afford to have a thought in my head about me that He doesn't have in His head about me. Thinking independently of God is not freedom. In fact, it is the worst possible bondage imaginable to think outside of the purpose and design set in place by the greatest creative genius ever to exist. The mind-boggling challenge comes when we realize that this One who owes us nothing has invited us into a co-laboring role in caring for all He has made through the privileged relationship of discovering His heart. As a result, the greatest gift we can give ourselves is to require that our thought life work in tandem with His goodness. Being tethered to His goodness is the most wonderful illustration of freedom and liberty possible.

THE ORIGINAL DESIGN[1]

The backbone of Kingdom authority and power is found in our *commission*. Kris Vallotton, who has been a dear friend and partner in ministry for the last thirty-eight years, puts it this way: "When you're in *sub*mission to His primary mission, you become *com*missioned." Discovering God's original commission and purpose for mankind can help to fortify our resolve to a life of history-shaping significance. To find that truth, we must go back to the beginning.

> **I can't afford to have a thought in my head about me that He doesn't have in His head about me.**

Man was created in the image of God and placed into the Father's ultimate expression of beauty and peace—the Garden of Eden. Outside of that garden, it was a different story. It was without the order and blessing contained within and was in great need of the touch of God's delegated one—Adam. It's an amazing thought to consider that something could be so perfect and good from God's perspective, yet be incomplete. God Himself longed to see what those who worshiped by choice would do with what He gave them to steward.

Adam and Eve were placed in the Garden with a mission. God said, *"Be fruitful and multiply; fill the earth and subdue it"* (Gen. 1:28). This was the first commission given to mankind. *"Be fruitful."*

This is a specific command to be productive. It included discovering the laws of God's creation and cooperating with them to make the ever-expanding Garden a better place. God was not afraid of their personalizing His creation. Their mark of delegated authority was to be seen in their management of creation itself.

"Multiply." They were to have children, who in turn would have children, and so on. It was God's intention that as they bore more children, who also lived under God's rule, they would be able to extend the boundaries of His Garden through the simplicity of their devotion to Him. Because they were His delegated authority, they could display the beauty of God's Kingdom by representing Him well. The greater the number of people in right relationship to God, the greater the impact of their leadership. This process was to continue until the entire earth was covered with the glorious rule of God through man.

"Fill the earth." This statement reveals that God's target was the entire planet. One can only imagine what that might have looked like had Adam and Eve not sinned—humanity living in perfect harmony, under One God, all working to glorify God through their management of what He had created. Every corner of the earth was to feel the influence of His delegated ones, who served and ruled out of love—love for God, love for one another, and love for all that He had made.

"Subdue it." This statement reveals something that is often ignored. The Garden of Eden was perfect. But the rest of the planet was in disarray. Outside of the Garden was chaos and disorder as it was under the influence of the devil and his hordes. For that reason, a military term was used to describe Adam and Eve's assignment. In a sense, they were born into a war. They were to bring the earth under their control and ultimately under the influence of God through their righteous rule.

Because satan had rebelled and had been cast out of Heaven with a portion of the fallen angels and had taken dominion of the earth, it becomes obvious why the rest of the planet needed to be subdued—it was under the influence of the powers of darkness. (See Genesis 1:2.) God could have destroyed the devil and his host with a word; instead He chose to defeat darkness through His delegated authority—those made in His image who were lovers of God by choice.

A ROMANCE STORY

The Sovereign One placed us—Adam's children—in charge of planet Earth, even though we were only capable of managing a small portion to start with. He did something similar to the children of Israel when He gave them all of the Promised Land. He basically told them, "It's all yours, although I'll give it to you little by little." He then went on to explain that the timing of the release of their inheritance was for their sake, so the beasts of the field wouldn't become too numerous for them. This is remarkable. From day one, God has longed for His people to rule out of their right relationship with Him. The centurion brilliantly illustrates this same principle when He asks Jesus to heal his servant in Matthew 8:7–10:

> **God could have destroyed the devil and his host with a word; instead He chose to defeat darkness through His delegated authority—those made in His image who were lovers of God by choice.**

Jesus said to him, "I will come and heal him." But the centurion said, "Lord, I am not worthy for You to come under my roof, but just say the word, and my servant will be healed. For I also am a man under authority, with soldiers under me; and I say to this one, 'Go!' and he goes, and to another, 'Come!' and he comes, and to my slave, 'Do this!' and he does it." Now when Jesus heard this, He marveled and said to those who were following, "Truly I say to you, I have not found such great faith with anyone in Israel."

Because the centurion was under authority, he knew he had authority. Adam and Eve were given a huge assignment, which depended on their relationship with God, not their gifts and talents alone. Their authority was based entirely on being under the authority of the Almighty God. This takes us back to a statement made earlier in this chapter: "When you're in submission to His primary mission, you become commissioned. God's mission is to be embraced and represented well by those who love Him by choice, bringing all that He has made back into its proper place.

"The heaven, even the heavens, are the Lord's; but the earth He has given to the children of men" (Ps. 115:16). This highest of honors was given to us because love always chooses the best. That is the beginning of the romance of our creation—created in His image, for intimacy, that dominion might be expressed through love. It is from this revelation that we are to learn to walk as His ambassadors, thus defeating the "prince of this world" (see John 14:30; Eph. 2:2). The stage was set for all of darkness to fall as man exercised his godly influence over creation. But instead, man fell.

THE FALL

Satan didn't come into the Garden of Eden and violently take possession of Adam and Eve. He couldn't—He had no dominion there. Dominion empowers. And because man was given the keys of dominion over the planet, the devil would have to get his authority from man. The suggestion to eat the forbidden fruit was simply the devil's effort to get Adam and Eve to agree with him in opposition to God, thus empowering him. To this day, it is through agreement that the devil is able to *kill, steal, and destroy.* He is still empowered through man's agreement.

Mankind's authority to rule was forfeited when Adam ate the forbidden fruit. Paul said, *"You are that one's slaves whom you obey"* (Rom. 6:16). In that one act, mankind went from ruler over a planet to the slave and possession of the evil one. All that Adam owned, including the title deed to the planet with its corresponding position of rule, became part of the devil's spoil. God's predetermined plan of redemption immediately kicked into play: *"I will put enmity between you and the woman, and between your seed and her seed; he shall bruise your head, and you shall bruise His heel"* (Gen. 3:15). Jesus would come to reclaim all that was lost.

There Were No Shortcuts to His Victory

God's plan of rulership for man never ceased. Jesus came to bear man's penalty for sin and recapture what had been lost. Luke 19:10 records that Jesus came *"to seek and to save that which was lost."* Not only was mankind lost to sin, his dominion over planet Earth was also lost. Jesus came to recapture *all* that was lost.

Satan tried to ruin that plan many times during Jesus' life. The first and most notable effort happened at the end of Jesus' forty-day fast. The devil was kicked out of Heaven because he considered himself equal to God and deserving of worship. And while he knew he wasn't worthy of Jesus' worship, he also knew that Jesus had come to reclaim the authority that man had given away. Satan had those keys. He said to Jesus, *"All this authority I will give You, and their glory; for this has been delivered to me, and I give it to whomever I wish.*

Therefore, if You will worship before me, all will be Yours" (Luke 4:6).
Notice the phrase *"for this has been delivered to me."* Satan could not
steal it. It had been relinquished when Adam abandoned God's rule.
It was as though satan was saying to Jesus, "I know what You came
for. You know what I want. Worship me, and I'll give the keys back."
In effect, satan offered Jesus a shortcut to His goal of recapturing
the keys of authority that man lost through sin. Jesus said "no" to
the shortcut and refused to give him any honor. (It was this same
desire for worship and self-promotion that caused satan's fall from
Heaven in the first place. See Isaiah 14:13.) Jesus held His course, for
He had come to die.

The Father wanted satan defeated by man, one made in His
image. Many make the mistake of thinking that the devil is the
opposite of God. He's a created being and would be more likely
compared to the opposite of Michael, also an archangel. The devil
has never been a threat to God in any possible measure. He can be
removed forever with a simple word. But God, in His wisdom, has
chosen to use the devil as a chess piece on a chessboard. He uses
him at will, so that the devil's best attempts to destroy are always
placed into the hands of the One who causes *"all things to work
together for good to those who love God, to those who are called according to His purpose"* (Rom. 8:28). We must remember God is building
for eternity—that is where the ultimate vindication and restoration
will be seen. Thankfully, there is a great measure of victory in this
life that is far beyond what any of us could earn. But it would be a
great mistake to ignore eternity, as eternity is the cornerstone of all
logic and reason.

Jesus, who would shed His blood to redeem mankind, emptied
Himself of His rights as God and took upon Himself the limitations
of man. While Jesus never stopped being God, He took on flesh to
complete the assignment that we failed to finish. Satan was defeated

by a man—the Son of Man—who was rightly related to God. Now, as people receive the work of Christ on the cross for salvation, they become grafted into that victory. Jesus defeated the devil with His sinless life, defeated him in His death by paying for our sins with His blood, and defeated him again in the resurrection, rising triumphant with the keys of authority over all, including death, hell, and the grave.

WE ARE BORN TO RULE

In redeeming man, Jesus recovered what man had given away. From the throne of triumph He declared, *"All authority has been given to Me in heaven and on earth. Go therefore"* (Matt. 28:18). In other words: *I got the keys back. Now go use them and reclaim what was lost.* In this passage, Jesus fulfills the promise He made to the disciples when He said, *"I will give you the keys of the kingdom of heaven"* (Matt. 16:19). The original plan was never aborted; it was fully realized once and for all in the resurrection and ascension of Jesus. We were then to be completely restored to His plan of ruling as a people made in His image. And as such, we would learn how to enforce the victory obtained at Calvary: *"The God of peace will soon crush Satan under your feet"* (Rom. 16:20).

> Eternity is the cornerstone of all logic and reason.

We were born to rule—rule over creation, over darkness—to plunder hell, to rescue those headed there, and to establish the rule of Jesus wherever we go by preaching the Gospel of the Kingdom. *Kingdom* means *King's domain, King's dominion.* In the original purpose of God, mankind ruled over creation. Now that sin has entered the world, creation has been infected by darkness, such as disease, sickness, afflicting spirits, poverty, natural disasters, and demonic influence. Our rule is still over creation, but now it is focused on exposing and undoing the works of the devil. We are to give what we have received to reach that end. (See Matthew 10:8.) If I truly receive power from an encounter with the God of power, I am equipped to give it away. The invasion of God into impossible situations comes through people who have received power from on high and have learned to release it into the circumstances of life.

THE KEY OF DAVID

The Gospel of salvation is to touch the whole man: Spirit, soul, and body. John G. Lake called this a *Triune Salvation*. A study on the word *evil* confirms the intended reach of His redemption. That word is found in Matthew 6:13: *"Deliver us from evil"* (KJV). The word *evil* represents the entire curse of sin upon man. *Poneros,* the Greek word for "evil," came from the word *ponos,* meaning "pain." And that word came from the root word *penes,* meaning "poor." Look at it: *Evil*—sin, *pain*—sickness, and *poor*—poverty. Jesus destroyed the power of sin, sickness, and poverty through His redemptive work on the cross. In Adam and Eve's commission to subdue the earth, they were without sin, sickness, and poverty. Now that we are restored to His original purpose, should we expect anything less? After all, this is called the better covenant!

We were given *"the keys to the Kingdom"* (see Matt. 16:19)—which in part is the authority *"to trample over all the powers of hell"* (see Luke 10:19). There is a unique application of this principle found in the phrase *"key of David,"* which is mentioned in both Revelation and Isaiah (see Rev. 3:7; Is. 22:22). *Unger's Bible Dictionary* states, "The power of the keys consisted not only in the supervision of the royal chambers, but also in deciding who was and who was not to be received into the King's service."[2] All that the Father has is ours through Christ. His entire treasure house of resources, His royal chambers, is at our disposal in order to fulfill His commission. But the more sobering part of this illustration is found in *controlling who gets in to see the King*. Isn't that what we do with this Gospel? When we declare it, we give opportunity for people to come to the King to be saved. When we are silent, we have chosen to keep those who would hear away from eternal life. Sobering indeed! It was a costly key for Him to purchase, and it's a costly key for us to use. But, it's even more costly to *bury it and not obtain an increase for the coming King*. That price will be felt throughout eternity.

A REVOLUTION IN IDENTITY

It's time for a revolution in our vision. When prophets tell us, *"Your vision is too small,"* many of us think the antidote is to increase whatever numbers we're expecting. For example: If we're expecting ten new converts, let's change it to one hundred. If we were praying for cities, let's pray instead for nations. With such responses, we're missing the sharp edge of the frequently repeated word. Increasing the numbers is not necessarily a sign of a larger vision from God's perspective. Vision starts with identity and purpose. Through a revolution in our identity, we can think with divine purpose. Such a change begins with a revelation of Him.

One of the tragedies of a weakened identity is how it affects our approach to Scripture. Many, if not most, theologians make the mistake of taking all the *good stuff* contained in the prophets and sweeping it under that mysterious rug called *the Millennium*. It is not my desire to debate that subject right now. But I do want to challenge our thinking and deal with our propensity to put off those things that require courage, faith, and action to another period of time. The mistaken idea is this: If it is good, it can't be for now.

A cornerstone in this theology is that the condition of the Church will always be getting worse and worse; therefore, tragedy in the Church is just another sign of these being the last days. In a perverted sense, the weakness of the Church confirms to many that they are on the right course. The worsening condition of the world and the Church becomes a sign to them that all is well. I have many problems with that kind of thinking, but only one I'll mention now—*it requires no faith!*

We are so entrenched in unbelief that anything contrary to this worldview is thought to be of the devil. So it is with the idea of the Church having a dominating impact before Jesus returns. It's almost as though we want to defend the right to be small in number and make it by the *skin of our teeth.* Embracing a belief system that requires no faith is dangerous and is in itself a contradiction in terms. It is contrary to the nature of God and all that the Scriptures declare. He plans to do *"above all we could ask or think,"* according to Ephesians 3:20, so His promises by nature challenge our intellect and expectations. "[Jerusalem] *did not consider her destiny; therefore her collapse was awesome"* (Lam. 1:9). The result of forgetting our destiny and His promises is not one we can afford.

We are often more convinced of our *unworthiness* than we are of His *worth.* Our *inability* takes on greater focus than does His *ability.* But the same One who called *fearful Gideon* a "valiant warrior" and *unstable Peter* a "rock" has called us the Body of His beloved Son on earth. That has to count for something. The very fact that He declares it makes the impossible possible.

Those who walk in arrogance because of how they see themselves in Christ don't really see it at all. When we see who He is, what He has done on our behalf, and who He says we are, there is only one possible response—worship from a humble and surrendered heart.

WORTH THE RISK

God didn't create us to be robots. He made us to be powerful expressions of Himself. When He did this, He made it possible for Him to feel heartache and pain from our choices. All parents understand this pain. He took a risk by giving us a choice to serve Him, ignore Him, or even mock Him. The Perfect One chose vulnerability, a willingness to be influenced by what He has made, over the squeaky clean world that the robots could manage without disrupting His plan. Why did He consider it worth the risk? What was He looking for? People, those made in His image, who took their place before Him as worshipers, as sons and daughters, as those whose very natures are immersed in His. They would become co-laborers in managing, creating, and contributing to the well-being of all He has made. From His perspective, it was worth the risk.

> **God has chosen to veil Himself in just the right measure so that our wills and intellects could be shaped by our allegiance to Him.**

Our freedom of choice is so valuable to Him that He restrains Himself from manifesting His presence in a way where our freedom of choice would be removed. That may sound strange to some, but when He reveals Himself in fullness, even the devil and his demons will declare that Jesus Christ is Lord. Some realities are so overwhelming, like the full manifestation of God's glory, that there's little room for reason and choice. God has chosen to veil Himself in just the right measure so that our wills and intellects could be shaped by our allegiance to Him. He is there for anyone humble enough to recognize his or her personal need. He is also subtle enough to be ignored by those who are filled with themselves.

HIS PASSION FOR OUR FREEDOM

Liberty, then, is not doing as we please. It's having the ability to do what is right. Real freedom is given to the humble because pride restricts, restrains, and leads to smallness. Liberty is the result of being freed by the Holy Spirit Himself, who demonstrates the fruits and benefits of coming under the Lordship of Jesus Christ. What an adventure! There's more room in the Kingdom of God than outside it. There's more freedom under His rule than there is in doing as I please. This is the kingdom where we rise by going low, receive by giving, and live by dying. What a kingdom indeed!

CREATION AND THE CREATOR

The enemy of our souls wars against everything that leads to true freedom. One of the great tragedies of this present day is that for the most part, our educational systems have succeeded in removing the concept of a creator from people's way of thinking and daily lifestyle. In doing so, society abandons its moral compass and loses the awareness of a code to live by. The moral compass is then replaced by what is popular in the moment, which constantly changes according to whoever has the microphone. Political correctness is the outcome. And it is here we find the evidence that stupidity is contagious. Insanity becomes flaunted as sanity, and the absence of moral responsibilities then becomes the doctrine of the day.

Consider this: When there is no creator, there is no design. When the concept of design is removed from our thinking and our lifestyles, then we lose the sense of purpose. When purpose is out of the equation, so also is the idea of an eternal destiny. And by removing eternity from the thoughts of a people, we also lose the sense of accountability. And when accountability is gone, so is the fear of the Lord. And *the fear of the Lord is the beginning of wisdom* (Ps.

111:10; Prov. 9:10). It's important at this point to emphasize that the fear of the Lord is significantly different than many interpret. It's not a fear that drives us from God, but one that draws us to Him. It is endearing in nature, and it is as essential for New Testament believers as it was in the Old Testament. This is wisdom. Wisdom is the essential building block for us to be able to fulfill our reason for being. Understanding how God created us and the purpose for our creation goes a long way in our correctly interpreting life on this planet without mistakenly questioning the goodness of God whenever we see a problem.

For some, this may seem like a giant too big to kill—an insurmountable task. Not so. All *ism's*, whether it's socialism, communism, Hinduism, Buddhism, or the like, cower in the face of an authentic Gospel, one of purity and power. Live it as Jesus lived it, say it as Jesus said it, and display it as Jesus displayed it. People will abandon everything inferior if they can but taste and see from the authentic Gospel of the Kingdom.

NOTES

1   Much of the remainder of this chapter was adapted from my book *When Heaven Invades Earth*, Chapter 2. Used with permission.

2.   *Unger's Bible Dictionary* (Chicago: Moody Press, 1957), 629.

Chapter Three

PURPOSE OF THE OLD TESTAMENT

If the whole universe has no meaning, we should
never have found out that it has no meaning: just as,
if there were no light in the universe and therefore
no creatures with eyes, we should never know it
was dark. Dark would be without meaning.

—C.S. LEWIS, *Mere Christianity*

I remember growing up thinking that God the Father was angry, and it was Jesus who calmed Him down. The stories of the Old Testament only seemed to confirm that misguided idea. It almost seemed like there were two completely different deities in charge of each dispensation. While that is not true, we've been left with a challenging task of reconciling the unique approaches to problems that couldn't be more diametrically opposed to each other than they are in the Old and New Testaments. And while there are glimpses of grace in the Old, it is the ongoing judgments, diseases, curses, and the like that all seem to have God's blessing, that become a theological nightmare—at least for me. I will admit that many people seem to have no problem with the conflict, but in all honesty, I refuse to embrace their theology. For the most part their concept of God violates all that Jesus Christ stood for and modeled for us to follow. And that really is the reason behind this book. There must be a better approach.

THE BEAUTY OF SCRIPTURE

I absolutely love ALL of Scripture! I have a special fondness for the Old Testament. If you can read and embrace it without being offended at God or using it to replace the standard that Jesus set in the New Testament, then it becomes a most glorious journey. Discovering the role of the Old in the days of the New is absolutely needed so that we might live in wisdom.

I realize that it is impossible to fully describe the beauty, wonder, and purpose of the Old Testament in such a small book, let alone a single chapter. The following is to help the reader to understand the high points of the Lord's targets in inspiring such wonder as the writing of Old Covenant Scripture. It remains a rich resource for the instruction of the New Testament believer.

Below are four of the main things that the Old Testament does for us that are helpful in recognizing and living in the goodness of God. The Old Testament:

1. Reveals the severity of sin.

2. Exposes the absolute hopeless condition of humanity to save itself.

3. Shows us our need of a savior.

4. Points to Jesus as the only possible solution to our lost condition.

THE SEVERITY OF SIN

Sin is so severe that it is terminal in every single case. It cannot be overlooked. The presence and power of sin have scarred all that God has made. No one can survive the effects of sin. The apostle Paul explains the role of the Law as it pertains to sin: *"where there is no law there is no transgression"* (Rom. 4:15). God does nothing to create shame in us. All that He reveals to us He does out of His goodness so that we might respond to His provision and become free. Without knowing our need, it's impossible to recognize His answer. When He reveals our absolute lost condition because of sin, He does so that we might turn from sin and receive His solution—forgiveness unto adoption.

The Law drives this point home over and over again by illustrating how sin contaminates everything it touches. For example, if you touch a leper in the Old Testament, you are unclean, requiring a process to become clean again. If you are bringing a lamb to be sacrificed, and somebody spits on it, the offering is now unclean. The idea is driven home page after page as the severity of sin must be realized to effectively turn from it unto God. The point is, under the Old Covenant unclean things affect the clean things. Sin contaminates.

> **When He reveals our absolute lost condition because of sin, He does so that we might turn from sin and receive His solution—forgiveness unto adoption.**

HOPELESS CONDITION OF HUMANITY

The Old Testament gives us an awareness of our sinfulness, revealing that we can't just decide not to sin anymore. It has become our nature. No amount of discipline or determination can change our bent toward sin, nor can it rid us of our sinful past. One of the more sobering realizations is that there is no number of good works that can make up for our sins. Self-help programs might help with losing weight or learning new skills. But they cannot touch the human dilemma called sin. It is out of the reach of all human efforts. Seeing that we are lost—completely lost—helps us to see our need of a savior.

Because sin contaminates all it touches, Israel had to destroy the surrounding nations when they entered the Promised Land. There was nothing put into place that could change the bent toward sin of the people who once occupied their inheritance. The only answer was their death; otherwise, their sinful nature would contaminate the work that God was doing in His own people. That's quite a difference from the Old Covenant to the New, where we are commanded to take this Good News to the surrounding nations and seek for their conversion.

WE NEED A SAVIOR

Seeing that we are utterly lost helps to open us up to outside help. And that outside help is from God Himself. The stubborn insistence that we provide for ourselves and take care of ourselves might help in some parts of life. But that trait is completely useless as it pertains to our need of salvation. Because we are lost, we must be found. In reality, none of us can "find Jesus." The Bible describes us as dead (separate from God). And dead people can't find a savior. Strangely, this provides the backdrop for all of us, as it pertains to our salvation. Those who are seeking God are simply responding to the summons of God that has been released over their hearts. We were found. Jesus called us by name, bringing conviction of sin into our lives. We responded and were born again—we came to life.

THE LAW POINTS TO JESUS

The Old Testament Law is the teacher that leads us to Christ. It first reveals that we are sinners; but, thankfully, it doesn't leave us there. *"Therefore the Law has become our tutor to lead us to Christ, so that we may be justified by faith. But now that faith has come, we are no longer under a tutor"* (Gal. 3:24–25). Jesus not only satisfied the appetite of the Law in bearing our judgment upon Himself; He was the One the Law was pointing to, much like a sign on a restaurant that points to what's inside the building. The Mosaic Law pointed to Jesus. There are many wonderful books that help to identify how the sacrifices, the feasts, the furniture of the Tabernacle of Moses, the Sabbath and Jubilee, and countless other things point to the coming of Jesus. That doesn't even count the prophecies that specifically announce the details of His life and His death. It was clearly announced to help His people recognize Him when He came. Tragically, many of the ones who were the most trained in the study of Scripture missed Jesus when He came. Their increased knowledge insulated them from their own needs and didn't lead them to a tender heart.

As you read and reread Old Testament Scriptures, it becomes obvious that the Father wanted us to realize that His answer was on the way. The Savior was on the way.

Because the Old Testament leads us to Jesus, it automatically points to the Kingdom that this King of kings rules over. The Kingdom is the realm of His rule, displaying His will for all He has made. Page after page carries the wonderful picture of the Kingdom of God that was to come. Throughout the time before Christ, there were events, prophecies, and laws that spoke of life under grace. There were unusual moments of grace that gave insight into what was coming through *types and shadows*. And while Israel expected the Kingdom to show up through the military rule of their Messiah, Jesus revealed it as a kingdom that first touched the heart:

> *Now when He was asked by the Pharisees when the kingdom of God would come, He answered them and said, "The kingdom of God does not come with observation; nor will they say, 'See here!' or 'See there!' For indeed,* **the kingdom of God is within you** (Luke 17:20–21).

This passage is an important clarification for all. The Kingdom doesn't come to be measured outwardly, though it has a profound effect on things that are visible, for example, the healing and deliverance of the body. (See Matthew 12:28.) Jesus is responding to people's expectation of the visible manifestation of the Kingdom through military force. It is a given that throughout Jesus' earthly life, miracles with the human body became evidence that the Kingdom of God is a present reality.

As strange as it may sound, none of the miracles of Jesus were given as a *public relations* move. In other words, they were not done to promote His ministry or to prove He had power. They all came out of His compassion for people, not to satisfy the need of onlookers for supernatural entertainment. The Scriptures carry warnings for those who become mere observers of the supernatural without the change that can only happen through repentance. The Kingdom comes first to rule over and heal our hearts, and then to affect all things outwardly. Another passage that helps with this point is found in Romans 14:17: *"For the kingdom of God is not eating and drinking, but righteousness and peace and joy in the Holy Spirit."* In other words, the Kingdom of God is not food or drink—outward things. Instead, it is entirely that which is unseen, in the heart—righteousness, peace, and joy. And while those things are inward issues, they quickly become manifest outwardly. It's hard to keep joy unseen. The prosperity of soul spoken of in 3 John 2 reveals how a healthy inward lifestyle affects our health, finances, and our overall well-being.

> **None of the miracles of Jesus were given as a *public relations* move. They all came out of His compassion for people, not to satisfy the need of onlookers for supernatural entertainment.**

The very word for *salvation* was never meant to mean "forgiveness of sin" alone. It is a word that means "wholeness, forgiveness, healing, and deliverance." Look at the Romans passage about the Kingdom—righteousness, peace, and joy (see Rom. 14:17). Righteousness deals with the sin issue, peace answers the deliverance/torment issue, and joy is the answer for sickness and disease, as in *"laughter is good medicine"* (see Prov. 17:22).

THE NEW FULFILLS THE OLD

Wonderful revelations are gained about life under the New Covenant from the Old Testament through types and shadows, meaning there are natural illustrations of spiritual truths. For example, we know that the Jews were required to offer a spotless lamb as a payment for their sin. But we also know that Jesus is the actual Lamb of God who takes away the sin of the world. Once the actual comes in answer to the Old Testament type or shadow, there's no more need to go back and embrace the symbol. Otherwise, animal sacrifices would still have merit.

The entire Old Testament points to Jesus. He is the central figure of ALL Scripture. Both the Law and the Prophets declared His role as Messiah, showing how Jesus would fulfill God's redemptive plan. The stories, prophecies, and laws all pointed to Him at various levels in the same way that a highway sign points to an upcoming city from varying distances. The sign is real and significant, but in itself, it is not the reality we are looking for. It points to something greater than itself. In this case, we must not worship the sign of the Old Testament; nor can we afford to be distracted by it, as though in some way it contained a greater reality than the message of the Messiah Himself. These signs serve their purpose by taking us to Jesus. A freeway sign never defines the city, and nor should the Old Testament be made to redefine who Jesus is. He is the fulfillment of both the Law and the Prophets. The nature of His life and purpose is clear and must not be diluted or dismantled by unresolved questions from the Old Covenant. Why did He come? He came to *destroy* the works of the devil.

> **We must not confuse our destiny with our assignment. Heaven is my destiny, while bringing the Kingdom is my assignment.**

THE NATURE OF THE MESSAGE

The Law and the Prophets were until John. Since that time the kingdom of God has been preached and everyone is pressing into it (Luke 16:16).

"Until John" is a very significant phrase, but one that seems to be mostly ignored. Both the Law and the Prophets were *trumped* by a

greater message, the Gospel of the Kingdom. One is the prevailing message while the other is obsolete, having been fulfilled. One has Heaven's backing; the other doesn't. One reveals God's purpose in this present day, defining our assignment; the other does not.

A message creates a reality. The nature of the message we carry determines the nature of the reality we will live and minister in. Those who fully embrace our God-given assignment for the message of the Kingdom will see the ever-increasing government of God displayed in the affairs of mankind. This is the only message that creates an environment suitable to the display of God's love, His uncompromising purity, and His unfathomable power. This is the message that Jesus preached and in turn taught His disciples to preach. It remains the *now word*.

The Church has largely replaced the Gospel of the Kingdom with the Gospel of salvation. It's the beauty of the salvation message that makes it so easy to miss the fact that it is only a part of the whole message that Jesus gave us. The Gospel of salvation is focused on getting people saved and going to Heaven. The Gospel of the Kingdom is focused on the transformation of lives, cities, and nations through the effect of God's present rule—this is made manifest by bringing the reality of Heaven to earth. We must not confuse our destiny with our assignment. Heaven is my destiny, while bringing the Kingdom is my assignment. The focus of the Kingdom message is the rightful dominion of God over everything. Whatever is inconsistent with Heaven—namely, disease, torment, hatred, division, and sin habits—must come under the authority of the King. These kinds of issues are broken off of people's lives because inferior realms cannot stand wherever the dominion of God becomes manifest. As we succeed in displaying this message, we are positioned to bring about cultural change in education, business, politics, the environment, and the other essential issues that we face today. This creates a most unusual phenomenon: The fruit of revival becomes the fuel of revival. And as long as we stay true to the message, the movement increases unto reformation.

The Kingdom is the message we're to carry forth into the nations of the world. (See Matthew 10:7 and Acts 28:31.) Our message is Jesus, who demonstrated what His world is like through words and actions.

There is no sickness in Heaven. When the Kingdom is manifest in a person's body, he is healed. (See Matthew 4:23.) There are no demons in Heaven, which is why deliverance is normal when Jesus touches people. (See Matthew 12:28.) It's all about what His world looks like, and how that reality can affect this one. The Kingdom of God is in the unseen realm and obviously is eternal. (See 2 Corinthians 4:17.) Perception is vital, so live with the realization that faith sees. Our conversion opens up that capacity to us all. *"Unless one is born again he cannot see the kingdom of God"* (John 3:3). The impact of His Kingdom in the here and now goes beyond these two illustrations, having effect on every area of life—both internally (soul) and externally. The point is that the Kingdom is to be preached and displayed so that all might know of His goodness in this life. Jesus illustrated this perfectly.

WHEN HEAVEN WAS SILENT

Why did Jesus say, *"until John"*? Why didn't He say, "until Jesus"? Because John was the one who broke Heaven's silence with the message of the Kingdom. Before John the Baptist came on the scene, there were four hundred years without one word from God. Heaven was silent. No visions, dreams, or prophecies. Nothing. Four hundred years of absolute silence, and then came John. The Holy Spirit is not carelessly highlighting this detail that the Law and the

Prophets were until John because it was John who first declared, *"Repent, for the kingdom of heaven is at hand!"* (Matt. 3:2). John was the one who announced the shift in Heaven's focus.

There is another place in Scripture where four hundred years is unusually significant. Understanding the first mention of this phrase, *four hundred years*, will help us to understand its importance in this case. Israel lived in Egypt as a nation of slaves for four hundred years. And then the divine moment came when everything changed. It was when the blood from a lamb was put on the doorpost of each Jewish home on the night specified by God. The Angel of the Lord came and released Israel from their slavery in Egypt to their destiny as a Promised Land people. In one moment, they went from being slaves to being free, from absolute poverty to possessing the wealth of the most prosperous nation in the world. It happened in a moment. The first mention of the phrase *four hundred years* resulted in the rescue of a people and the formation of a nation, Israel. This was the redemption of God's people. In the time of John the Baptist, God announced the rescue and creation of a new nation, declaring, "It's a new day!" This time it would be a nation formed in the Spirit through conversion, including people from every tribe and tongue on the planet. For the first time since Genesis 1, there would actually be a *"new creation"* (see 2 Cor. 5:17), which is a people *"born of the Spirit"* (see John 3:6–8).

> **Don't skip over the bigger promises of Scripture simply because they are hard to believe because of their size.**

That is exactly the message of Jesus in Luke 16:16. It's a new day! The new day is marked with a new message. One message is over, and another has begun. When John the Baptist came forth, it was even more significant than deliverance from four hundred years of slavery under Egypt. That deliverance dealt with the nature and potential of mankind, but John's pronouncement changed everything.

Jesus made the amazing statement, *"Now the kingdom of God is being preached and everyone is pressing into it"* (Luke 16:16). Is it possible that the nature of the message determines the size of the harvest? He did say *"everyone"!* While I do not believe in Universalism, where everyone eventually ends up in Heaven, the message of the Kingdom has a greater reach than I previously thought possible. This is the message: "His dominion is everlasting. It is NOW. Jesus' life demonstrated His dominion over everything that was inconsistent with God's will."

Don't skip over the bigger promises of Scripture simply because they are hard to believe because of their size. Whenever He declares something this big, He's hoping to capture people's hearts, making it impossible for them to be satisfied with mediocrity. Here He says, *"Everyone is pressing into it"* (Luke 16:16). In Joel 2:28, He says, *"I will pour out My Spirit on all flesh."* In Jeremiah 31:34, He states, *"And all shall know Me."* Psalm 22, the psalm that deals with the crucifixion of Christ more than any other, states, *"All the ends of the world shall remember and turn to the Lord, and all the families of the nations shall worship before You"* (Ps. 22:27). This list of extraordinary promises could continue page after page. But you get the point. The promises are there, in a sense waiting for adoption. Instead of trying to figure out the season for the promises to be fulfilled, why not come before God and see if God might want to fulfill them in our time? After all, how many times did the disciples get the timing right in their understanding of God's prophetic promises? I don't consider myself any better than they were. These promises are not given to us to help us to know the future as much as they are given to create hunger for what might be. The promises of God are clearly seen when the people of God get hungry and cry out to God for their fulfillment. This is exactly what Daniel did in reading Jeremiah's prophecy. (See Daniel 9:2–6.) He turned the prophecies into prayers for his generation.

When you declare the right message, you create the atmosphere where everyone is able to press in. No matter the need, there is an answer now. The right message marries the truth of Jesus as the *desire of the nations* with the nations themselves. The right message changes the atmosphere to make the manifestation of His dominion realized. Perhaps this is the context in which the irresistible grace of God is embraced, thus fulfilling the desire found in the heart of every person alive.

IT IS FINISHED

*After this, Jesus, knowing that all things were now accomplished, that the Scripture might be fulfilled, said, "I thirst!" ...So when Jesus had received the sour wine, He said, "**It is finished**!" And bowing His head, He gave up His spirit* (John 19:28–30).

It is a mistake to think that when Jesus cried out, *"It is finished,"* He was merely proclaiming that His life as a man living on earth was over. Both the Law and the Prophets had rightfully made a judgment on humanity, for God Himself declared, *"The person who sins shall die!"* (Ezek. 18:20). The power of this judgment was so strong that if Jesus had not come for one hundred thousand years, and trillions of people had lived during that time, it rightfully would have damned every single one and still not have been satisfied in its demands. Jesus came to quench the appetite of that unquenchable fire by meeting the requirements of the Law and the Prophets. When He said, *"It is finished,"* He was declaring, "The appetite of the Law and Prophets has been satisfied once and for all! It's a new day." As a result, we each go from a slave to a possessor of the Kingdom in a moment: Transferred from the kingdom of darkness to the Kingdom of light, from being the one who has no rights in God to suddenly being the eternal dwelling place of God Himself.

REPENTING ENOUGH TO SEE THE KINGDOM

"Repent, for the Kingdom of heaven is at hand" (Matt. 4:17). This word *repent* means "to change our way of thinking." But it is much more than a mental exercise. It really is the deep sorrow for sin that enables a person to truly repent and change his mind or perspective on reality. Hebrews 6:1 clearly teaches that there are two sides to this action: *"Repentance from dead works... faith toward God."* Full repentance is *from* something *toward* something—*from* sin *toward* God. Many Christians repent enough to be forgiven but not enough to see the Kingdom. Their repentance doesn't bring the Kingdom into view.

> **Many Christians repent enough to be forgiven but not enough to see the Kingdom.**

The same concept is taught with two different perspectives. One passage (Hebrews 6:1) says *"toward God"* and the other (Matthew 4:17) implies it's *"toward the Kingdom."* Luke captures the richness of both views when he writes: *"Repent therefore and be converted, that your sins may be blotted out, so that times of refreshing may come from the presence of the Lord"* (Acts 3:19). The point is *the presence is the Kingdom.* It really is that simple.

It's too easy to complicate the Christian life. For example, we are told to put on the full armor of God, which includes the helmet of salvation, breastplate of righteousness, and so on (see Eph. 6:10–18). The apostle Paul gave us this important instruction, but most of the time we miss the point. God *is* my armor. He's not saying,

"Put something on that is a reality that is separate from Me." He's saying, "I'm it. Just abide in Me. I become your salvation. I am your righteousness, the breastplate over you. I am the Gospel of peace. I am the Good News. I am the sword of the Spirit." This list paints a profound word picture, enabling us to realize the fuller benefit of abiding in Christ. Simple is better.

Jesus tells us to repent because He brought His world with Him. If I don't shift my perspective on reality, I will never discover the superior reality—the unseen realm of His dominion. This kind of repentance enables a believer to live in *"heavenly places in Christ"* (see Eph. 1:3). Discovering the presence of God is discovering the Kingdom.

Chapter Four

THE OLD HAS A NEW PURPOSE

The ultimate question is whether the doctrine of the goodness of God or that of the inerrancy of Scriptures is to prevail when they conflict. I think the doctrine of the goodness of God is the more certain of the two. Indeed, only that doctrine renders this worship of Him obligatory or even permissible.

—C.S. LEWIS

I love the Bible, the whole Bible, more than I have words to express. My personal study of the Scriptures has been spent in both the Old and New Testaments. I spent many years teaching primarily from the Old Testament Scriptures, as I discovered that they were the "root system" for what we enjoy in Christ. It was an essential part of my developing years. Seeing the purposes of God as revealed in His dealings with Israel and the surrounding nations has proven to be invaluable for me as I consider His design and purpose for the New Testament Church. It's been a glorious journey, one that continues to develop in beauty and purpose.

One of the passages that caught me early in life is the one found in Romans 15:4: *"For whatever was written in earlier times was written for our instruction, so that through perseverance and the encouragement of the Scriptures we might have hope."* This addresses the purpose for the study of the Old Testament. Please notice that correct study of Scripture is to give us encouragement that results in great hope—that we might have hope. And yet for many, the study of the Old Testament does anything but give them hope for their own lives. All many see are the judgments of God toward the nations. I believe if we get a different outcome than what this Romans passage said we would have (encouragement and hope), we must learn to approach the Scriptures differently until we bear His intended fruit.

The Old Testament was given for our instruction as New Covenant people. For a season, the Old Testament Scriptures were the only Bible that the New Testament Church had. What has been written gives us the backdrop to the truths we enjoy today. But as it is with most things, improper application can also bring death. *"For the letter kills, but the Spirit gives life"* (2 Cor. 3:6). It's a matter of perception. Many Christians' lives have been crippled because of an unclear understanding of what Jesus came to accomplish and fulfill. If I don't understand that, I won't understand my purpose and calling. To put it more practically, through wisdom and revelation we must understand what of the Old Testament *ended at the cross,* what *was changed by the cross,* and what *came through the cross unchanged.* Let me illustrate:

What ended at the cross: The sacrifice of animals was required under the Old Testament Law. It was mandated by God to remind us that the penalty of sin is death. And while the blood of animals never actually did away with the record of sin, dealt with the nature of sin in the ones making the sacrifice, or dealt with the consequences of sin, it did postpone the penalty for one more year. It became a point of obedience that prophesied of what was coming—the Lamb of God, who would take away the sins of the world. When Jesus offered Himself as a sacrifice on behalf of all mankind, He made it possible for the sacrifice of one to make the many righteous. (See Romans 5:19.) When Jesus Christ died on our behalf once and for all, it changed everything. He was the Lamb of God, without sin, blemish, or fault of any kind. The requirement of the Law for the shedding of blood for sin was satisfied for all time. We can say with confidence that never again will we be required to sacrifice another animal to postpone the penalty of sin for one more year. It is finished. The cross brought an end to the sacrifice of animals and, more importantly, satisfied the appetite of the Law for the judgment of humanity. Salvation is now given to all who call upon the name of the Lord.

What changed at the cross: The Sabbath was created for the benefit of mankind. It was an important enough part of God's economy that He Himself rested the seventh day from His works in creation. On the Sabbath, we are to rest on the seventh day from all our labors. God even required that the land rest every seven years (rest from planting crops). Then every seventh Sabbath year required yet another year of rest, this time marked by what the Bible calls the Year of Jubilee. So that means that both the forty-ninth and the fiftieth year, the land rests again, while at the same time debts are forgiven, slaves are freed, and many other similar things are done to increase the well-being of God's people. But as you can imagine, not planting crops that seventh year requires that His people trust Him to provide for them like He did for Israel in the wilderness.

They had to believe that God would take care of them through the growth of uncultivated crops—crops they did not replant from the previous year. And while I do think the weekly Sabbath rest is *essential* for mental, emotional, physical, and spiritual health, the Sabbath was also a foretaste of what the daily life of the believer is to be like—without works as it pertains to our salvation. Both the Sabbath and the Year of Jubilee were changed at the cross.

When Jesus announced the beginning of His ministry, He declared, *"The Spirit of the Lord is upon Me...to declare the favorable year of the Lord"* (Luke 4:18). That year is the Year of Jubilee! In essence, He was saying that the Year of Jubilee was the ongoing experience of those belonging to Him. The freedom that the Jubilee provides is to be the distinguishing mark on the lives of those who have met Jesus. The Scripture puts it this way: *"Now the Lord is the Spirit, and where the Spirit of the Lord is, there is liberty"* (2 Cor. 3:17). In other words, every day is the Sabbath and every year is the Year of Jubilee—rest and liberty are to be seen on the countenance of all who belong to Him. And while I don't think there are many who truly live the beauty of this truth, it is a reality of His Kingdom that is available to all. That being said, this is quite a change from the Old Testament—Jubilee changed from being every fifty years to now being the everyday lifestyle of those in Christ every year. The cross of Jesus brought about such change, suggesting that what existed before was a prototype of what was to come.

The Old Testament is filled with things that were prototypes, or prophetic glimpses of the future. And all of these things reveal layer after layer of the goodness of God that was to become more fully manifest on this side of the cross. Many get stuck on the harshness of the Old Testament stories at the expense of seeing the reality of His goodness that was displayed throughout history—much like a rose among thorns—but is now more fully manifest through the lifestyle illustrated by Jesus. It is, and has always been, about His goodness.

In summary, the cross changed the nature of rest and freedom. Both the Sabbath and the Jubilee were changed through the sacrifice of Jesus on our behalf. There's no sense ignoring what He bought for us to enjoy as the continuous, ongoing lifestyle of the disciple of Jesus.

What came through the cross unchanged: King David is known for many wonderful things throughout Scripture. He was a great king who led Israel into their greatest hour. He was a man after God's heart. He proved this long before He became king. Even his bravery was proven long before he was seated upon the throne. His courage against the lion and the bear when no one was watching set him up for the victory over Goliath when two entire nations were watching. This set the pace for His profound leadership with the people of God—one of extraordinary courage. But the one thing that was the primary reference point in all of his life was his passion for the presence of God. I think that his biggest mark on history was the standard he set as a worshiper. It was his worship that sculpted the heart of a nation into a nation who valued the presence of God. As Moses once declared, it was the presence of God upon His people that became the distinguishing mark that separated them from all other nations. (See Exodus 33:16.)

David was a worshiper on the backside of the desert caring for his father's sheep. This wasn't done for performance or status. It was the purest expression of his heart and became the reason for God choosing him above his brothers as the ruler over Israel.

When David became king, he wanted the Ark of the Covenant, the dwelling place of God among mankind, in his city of Jerusalem. So David pitched a tent on Mount Zion that housed the Ark of the Covenant. Mount Zion is a small rise in the earth within the city of Jerusalem. That is where the presence of God rested for the benefit of the whole nation of Israel. We don't know the size of the tent. All we know is that God was there, and so were the priests. They ministered to God through thanksgiving, praise, and worship with their musical instruments and physical expressions like raising their hands, bowing low, dancing, as well as lifting up their voices. The great honor for anyone, terrifying as it may have been, was to be able to come into the presence of the Almighty God. That very act was forbidden to them under the Law. But God in His mercy allowed them to taste of a New Testament reality long before its time. Under David, they did this daily. He had all the priests trained in music so they could lift up praises twenty-four hours a day, seven days a week. They took shifts so they could do this nonstop.

The priests had to shift their focus from the sacrifice of animals to the sacrifice of praise. Their role changed so dramatically that it would be hard for us to comprehend what it must have been like to serve under King Saul and then under David. The skills needed under one leader were completely useless under the next. They turned from the focus of keeping the Law to keeping the presence. An important feature to remember is that most of the time when the Bible talks about the presence of God, it's actually talking about His face. That is the meaning of the Hebrew word translated *presence*.

The prophet Amos declared that in the last days there would be a rebuilding of this Tabernacle of David. The time of the fulfillment of this word would be when the Gentiles were added to what God was doing on the earth—they, too, would become His people. After the Great Commission given to the Church by Jesus to *"go into all the world"* (Matt. 28:19), followed by the outpouring of the Holy Spirit that would help them be effective (see Acts 2), Gentiles began to be added to the Church. It became so controversial that the leaders of the church called a meeting in Jerusalem (see Acts 15). The conclusion of this gathering of apostolic leaders was that the inclusion of Gentiles to the faith was in fact from God. They were to be careful *not* to burden them with the requirements of the Law that they themselves could not keep. The Old Testament Scripture they used to support this idea was the Amos 9:11–12 passage:

> *"In that day I will raise up the fallen booth of David, and wall up its breaches; I will also raise up its ruins and rebuild it as in the days of old; that they may possess the remnant of Edom and all the nations who are called by My name," declares the Lord who does this.*

Notice that the rebuilding of this tabernacle, known for the abiding presence of God and the worship from the priests, coincides with Gentiles being added to the faith. There is a connection in the unseen realm between the effect of worship and the conversion of souls.

The Tabernacle of David changed the focus of life and ministry for all priests in the Old Testament. It's a good thing, too. In the New Testament, we discover that every believer is now a priest unto the Lord. (See 1 Peter 2:9.) The Old Testament priesthood would be impossible for a New Testament believer to emulate, as it was focused on the sacrifice of animals and the worship of God in one location—the tabernacle or temple, depending on the time period. So this Old Testament story is once again a prophetic prototype of what we are to become.

We now have the privilege of ministering to God as they did in David's tabernacle. And the beautiful thing for us all is that this wor- **Worship clears the airwaves.** ship can and must be done in our homes, our cars, as well as in the corporate gatherings with our brothers and sisters. Such a role has such a dramatic effect on the atmosphere here on earth that people become converted. My thinking is that the atmosphere in our homes and churches becomes so saturated with the glory of God in response to our worship that people are able to see and hear truth clearly. Worship clears the airwaves. In that sense, the Tabernacle of David, and its corresponding role in worship, is unchanged from the Old Testament to the New. Further study will again verify that the ministry of thanksgiving, praise, and worship—all aspects of our ministry unto Him—are all unchanged by the cross. In fact, it was the cross that brought this prototype out of the laboratory of an Old Testament experiment into the daily life of God's people, who have become His eternal dwelling place. It has become a norm.

ADJUSTMENTS

Making these adjustments will help believers not to make the mistake of misapplying Scripture to their lives. So many believers live under the curse of the Law because of taking the wrong approach to the Old Testament. This simple adjustment will help us live in the freedom that Jesus bought for us. For in living in freedom, we illustrate what He is like and model what living under His rule looks like. This is a huge part of our message of the Gospel—live it, and when necessary use words.

Chapter Five

HIS GOODNESS—HIS GLORY

You become like what you worship. When you gaze in awe, admiration, and wonder at something or someone, you begin to take on something of the character of the object of your worship.

—N.T. WRIGHT

The Law of Moses was but for a season. It was never meant to carry the full manifestation of God's nature to be discovered and enjoyed by His people. While it was necessary and beautiful, it fell far short in representing the Father's heart. That was not its purpose. The Law taught Israel what they needed to know about the Messiah before He came upon the scene. And even then, most missed His coming. And yet riddled all throughout God's dealings with His people in the Old Testament was the revelation of grace. Some of the most beautiful glimpses of God's heart are hidden in the scenes of the Old Testament. There are great differences between law and grace. But for now, this will suffice—law requires, while grace enables.

God illustrated His heart for His people over and over again. He declared, "Say to them, 'As I live!' declares the Lord God, 'I take no pleasure in the death of the wicked, but rather that the wicked turn from his way and live. Turn back, turn back from your evil ways! Why then will you die, O house of Israel?'" (Ezek. 33:11). God is not an angry tyrant wishing evil people to be punished and to die. If that were true, it would have happened long before now, released through a simple decree. Instead, we see Him interceding so that the wicked would turn and live. His passion for all of us is to experience life to the fullest! But it is never forced upon us; otherwise, He ends up with robots, not people made in His image.

One of the most treasured portions of Old Testament Scripture is the blessing God told Moses to pass on to Aaron to declare over His people. Obviously, God can bless whomever He wants, whenever He wants. But He longed for His people to know His heart for them. He also wanted it to be spoken, as something happens when we join our words with His heart.

Aaron was the high priest, and as such he was positioned to release the blessing of God over the people. God wanted blessing declared over His people every day of their lives. It was to be declared because what is spoken makes a difference. This was not simply a formality. Everything God tells us to do has great significance. This is a picture of the high priest joining his heart with the heart of God—to release the reality of His Kingdom into the lives of His people through decree. We live with the conviction that nothing happens in the Kingdom of God until something is spoken. This passage reveals His passion for His

Law requires, while grace enables.

people to know of His love, His bounty, and His all sufficiency. This is the heart of God for us all:

> Then the Lord spoke to Moses, saying, "Speak to Aaron and to his sons, saying, 'Thus you shall bless the sons of Israel. You shall say to them: The Lord bless you, and keep you; the Lord make His face shine on you, and be gracious to you; the Lord lift up His countenance on you, and give you peace.' So they shall invoke My name on the sons of Israel, and I then will bless them" (Numbers 6:22–27).

THE GOD JOURNEY

God invites us to discover Him, the One who rewards all who join in the journey into the great expanse called the goodness of God. This is the journey of faith, for faith believes *"that He is, and that He is the rewarder of those who seek Him"* (Heb. 11:6). Faith has two parts; the first is a conviction of His existence. But even the devil has that much going for him. It's the second part that launches us into the adventure and distinguishes us from the rest of all that exists—a confidence in His nature. He is a rewarder! In other words, what we believe about Him will have an effect on our lives in a measurable way because He rewards those who have set their hearts on discovering Him. He promises, *"You will seek Me...and I will be found by you!"* (Jer. 29:13–14). God ensures that we find Him if the heart is genuinely searching with a readiness to obey. Jesus also said He would disclose Himself to those who follow Him (see John 14:21).

What we believe about Him will have an effect on our lives in a measurable way because He rewards those who have set their hearts on discovering Him.

It's as though He is saying that if we seek Him with all of our hearts, He will make sure to put Himself in the middle of the road we're walking on.

This invitation comes from the Father of life—the eternal God who loves through sacrifice and giving. The greatest gift we could ever give ourselves is to anchor our intellect and will into the strongest foundation possible—the goodness of God.

This voyage is one of faith. Faith is considered to be anti-intellectual by many. It is not. In reality, it enhances the intellect but is vastly superior, for it is able to recognize the unseen world that the natural mind has little place for. Real faith is superior to the human intellect in that it is the product of God's mind instead of ours. Faith comes from the heart, one that lives under the influence of His mind. Faith is the result of surrender, not self-will. It's more correctly stated that our intellect is shaped and influenced by authentic faith, for true faith precedes understanding on eternal matters, like those pertaining to the unseen world. *"By faith we understand that the worlds were prepared by the word of God, so that what is seen was not made out of things which are visible"* (Heb. 11:3). Take note that it is faith that enables us to understand the unseen world, which according to the apostle Paul is eternal, while the things we see are temporal. (See 2 Corinthians 4:18.) So faith then anchors us into the substance of eternity, a solid footing for sure. By faith we understand, for it is faith that enhances the intellect.

My faith can go only where I have understanding of His goodness. His goodness then becomes the real estate that I live on and explore freely. He liberally gives us all He is and all He has. (See John 16:14–15.) Biblical faith explores this realm with the delight

> **Real faith is superior to the human intellect in that it is the product of God's mind instead of ours.**

and pleasure of a well-loved child. Jesus teaches that the Kingdom of God belongs to those who are like children. Adults tend to manage what they have, taking fewer and fewer risks as they get older. But children tirelessly explore. When our faith explores His goodness, we are most like the children Jesus honored and celebrated. (See Mark 10:14.)

THE ADVENTURE INTO THE EXTREME

Everything about God is extreme in the best possible sense. He is infinitely good, infinitely holy and powerful, infinitely beautiful, magnificent, and glorious. These are just a few terms to describe Him. But none of the endless lists of traits and characteristics confine Him. Religion, which I define as *form without power*, tends to attempt the impossible task of restricting Him into neat little packages, giving us a false sense of intelligence and ultimately control. But He is bigger and bigger and bigger still. Each virtue gives us a glimpse into that which is beyond measure but is open for observation. You could take one trait and explore it for all of eternity but not come close to exhausting the depths of who He is in that particular virtue.

My faith can go only where I have understanding of His goodness.

History is filled with the stories of explorers and their adventures. Whether it's the quest of a Columbus to go where no European had gone before, or the astronauts who travel through space, or the intellectually curious of our day exploring the depths of science, medicine, and technology, we have been given the drive to search for more. God invites us into these quests as a part of our God-given nature to discover and create. His gifts of curiosity and desire are beautiful expressions of His heart as a Father.

George Washington Carver used this drive to discover things that would ultimately help the poor he lived to serve. His passion to unveil the secrets of creation began with his research on the peanut. He was known for his absolute faith in God as the cornerstone of his research and is credited with discovering over three hundred uses for the peanut. He claimed that it was faith that "held all inquiry and action accountable."[1] The impact of his research reached far and wide, but his primary target was to benefit the poor. As a result, this one man is credited with having an amazing impact on the economy of the southern states in the US, all because he believed God rewards those who seek Him.

HIDE AND SEEK

Solomon, the man known for unequalled wisdom, made this declaration: *"It is the glory of God to conceal a matter, but the glory of kings is to search out a matter"* (Prov. 25:2). I find it fascinating that God is glorified by concealing or hiding things. But it must be understood that He hides things for us, not from us.

The Father draws us into the journey of discovering His nature. His entire realm of dominion called the Kingdom of God is hidden for us to find.

My wife Beni and I have nine grandchildren. On Easter we hide eggs for them in our front yard. While I've never been able to figure out what a bunny and eggs have to do with the resurrection of Jesus, we still love hiding eggs for the children in our lives. It is just another excuse to have fun with our family. That being said, I would never dig a three-foot hole in the ground, put in the various kinds of eggs we use into the bottom of the hole, and then cover it with cement. Can you imagine me telling our grandchildren, "If you think you're so smart, try to find those eggs"? Hardly. We hide the eggs to be found. There's no joy in putting something out of their reach. Our joy is in their discovery.

All the adults cheer for them to find what's been hidden. We yell out when they're close. We'll even tell them to turn this way or that, or look higher or lower. We would never think of going into the house while they hunt for these treasures outside. They have great joy in finding the eggs. But they also look back at us, making sure we are watching. Part of their joy is in our joy over them. Our grandchildren range from five to sixteen years of age. (The three oldest ones, fourteen to sixteen years old, now help the younger ones to be successful.) We put some eggs in very hard places and others out in the open. The older ones know that if the egg is "hidden in the open," it's for one of the younger ones. When they were two years old, we'd put the brightly colored treasures on the steps, or on the bricks, or on the driveway next to a car tire. The eggs were hidden in the open so they'd be found. But if we put all the eggs in the open, the older ones would have no fun at all. They'd rightfully complain about our lack of effort to make it challenging for them. Their maturity requires that we take more thought in where we hide the eggs. Remember, the goal is joy, fun, and pleasure in the context of family. This simple illustration wonderfully represents our discovery of His goodness and speaks of His delight in our discovery. He truly is glorified in concealing a matter for us to find.

In the same way, the Father draws us into the journey of discovering His nature. His entire realm of dominion called the Kingdom of God is hidden for us to find. It is an eternal kingdom in which all of eternity will be needed to discover what He has made for us.

The second part of the Proverbs 25:2 passage is equally important to the first part: *the glory of kings is to search out a matter.* We have been created in the image of God, the King of all kings. We are royalty. Our royalty is never more at the forefront of our lives than when we live with the conviction that God has given us legal access to all things, including the hidden things—mysteries. And so we ask, seek, and knock, knowing there will be a breakthrough. (See Matthew 7:7–8.) Some of the things in this kingdom are discovered almost without looking. They seem to find us. And yet other breakthroughs seem to take the better part of a lifetime. This joyful adventure begins now, but it will continue throughout all eternity.

THE LAND OF GOODNESS

We all are explorers, searching for the new, enjoying the old, becoming personally enlarged with each discovery. What we behold affects us. If we look at it long enough, it changes us. There are parts of God's goodness that are easily noticeable to the casual observer. Much like Moses, we've been given a challenge. He saw a burning bush that wasn't being consumed by its flames. The story records an important detail that should help us all in our journey. It was only when Moses turned aside that the Lord spoke to him from the bush. (See Exodus 3:4.) Sometimes giving undivided attention to the obvious releases a greater encounter with Him, manifesting a greater revelation of what He is like. The bottom line is that we can't find anything significant on our own. It must be revealed to us. In other words, all discoveries are not the result of our discipline and determination alone. As the ultimate steward, He gives these gifts to those who have embraced His invitation to ask, seek, and knock.

The prophet Jeremiah caught a glimpse of this reality when God gave him a promise of restoration. *"Call to Me and I will answer you, and I will tell you great and mighty things, which you do not know"* (Jer. 33:3). The God who is good gave us the invitation to call upon

Him. He then promised to answer in a way that was beyond what we asked for. The word *great* in this verse means "considerably above average." And if that weren't enough, He follows the word *great* with the word *mighty. Mighty* means "inaccessible." Consider this: God has given us access to the inaccessible. What an incomprehensible promise! It is out of the reach of our skills, character, or qualifications. We lack all that is necessary to be able to apprehend what exists in the realm called the goodness of God. But He gave us something that makes this impossibility possible. He gave us the key to the inaccessible. He Himself is that key. Through His name we have access to that which is beyond our reach on our best day. The invitation came from His goodness. He invites us to call upon Him, giving Him the open door to answer in a way that is above our expectations and imagination. There is no goodness apart from Him, so our journey

We were created and designed to live in the glory of God, which is the manifested presence of Jesus.

is a discovery of the person of God—the One whose inaccessible goodness is now accessible by an invitation with His promise *to be found by us.*

EXPLORERS UNITE!

Like the adventurers of old, we have before us the most unexplored territory in existence. It is more rugged than Mount Everest, more intimidating than the deepest ocean, and vaster than space itself—it's called God's goodness. We've been invited by God Himself to come taste and see. He has also given us a tour guide to lead and assist us in this journey—the Holy Spirit. He has been given to lead us into all truth, which is always to manifest in freedom.

Once again, we look to Moses, the one to whom the Law was given. In one of his encounters with God, we see an example of grace that creates a high watermark, even by New Testament standards. The apostle Paul mentioned it in 2 Corinthians 3:7–18, announcing that this glorious moment was less than what the New Covenant provided for each believer. The New Covenant is better than the Old, and therefore it must provide superior blessings and breakthroughs.

In Exodus 33, we find Moses asking God not to send an angel to go with Israel into the Promised Land. He wanted God Himself to go. In fact, Moses stated that if God wasn't going to go, then he didn't want to go, either. This really is quite remarkable. The angel assigned to lead them would have provided everything that God promised. It would have been a fulfillment of all their dreams and aspirations as a nation. And I remind you that angels carry a certain majesty and glory that is often mistaken for God Himself. Yet Moses had a relationship with God, forged through his trials. God said of Moses, *The Lord used to speak to Moses face to face, just as a man speaks to his friend* (Ex. 33:11). As a friend of God, Moses wanted only to be led by his friend. The blessings were not the objective, but the relationship was.

> *The Lord said to Moses, "I will also do this thing of which you have spoken; for you have found favor in My sight and I have known you by name." Then Moses said, "I pray You, **show me Your glory!**" And He said, "**I Myself will make all My goodness pass before you**, and will proclaim the name of the Lord before you; and I will be gracious to whom I will be gracious, and will show compassion on whom I will show compassion." But He said, "You cannot see My face, for no man can see Me*

and live!" Then the Lord said, "Behold, there is a place by Me, and you shall stand there on the rock; and it will come about, while My glory is passing by, that I will put you in the cleft of the rock and cover you with My hand until I have passed by. Then I will take My hand away and you shall see My back, but My face shall not be seen" (Exodus 33:17–23).

When Moses asked to see the glory of God, he did not choose some random aspect of God's person or nature. He chose the original target for every person alive. We were created and designed to live in the glory of God, which is the manifested presence of Jesus. The Scripture says, *"For all have sinned and fall short of the glory of God"* (Rom. 3:23). Sin caused us to fall short of God's intended target. *To sin* means "to miss the mark." Consider an archer shooting an arrow at a target and then watching that arrow not even reach the target, let alone hit the bull's-eye. That is what our sin has done. We not only missed the mark; we didn't even reach the target. But take note of the target—it is the glory of God. We were created to live in that realm. Moses knew it instinctively and longed to see it more clearly.

Consider all the encounters that Moses had with God. The glory of God was present in the burning bush, during the many times on the mountain where God descended upon Moses and spoke, and through the visitations in the tent of meeting, which was also filled with His glory. These are just a few of the examples listed in Scripture. Yet in this moment, there was only one thing in his mind—the glory. All of those encounters had an effect on Moses, and then upon Israel. Once you've tasted of the real reason that you're alive, nothing else will ever satisfy. But this particular encounter with God in His glory is the only time Moses' face shone like

God's. I think it's important to notice what was unique about this encounter. It's the only time people feared the appearance of Moses, and they had him put a cloth over his head to protect them from what they were seeing upon him. I have this deep personal sense that the glory of God will be a primary subject and passion of the Church in the coming years.

> *It came about when Moses was coming down from Mount Sinai (and the two tablets of the testimony were in Moses' hand as he was coming down from the mountain), that Moses did not know that **the skin of his face shone because of his speaking with Him.** So when Aaron and all the sons of Israel saw Moses, behold, **the skin of his face shone, and they were afraid to come near him.** Then Moses called to them, and Aaron and all the rulers in the congregation returned to him; and Moses spoke to them. Afterward all the sons of Israel came near, and he commanded them to do everything that the Lord had spoken to him on Mount Sinai. **When Moses had finished speaking with them, he put a veil over his face** (Exodus 34:29–33).*

Moses asked to see God's glory. God said "OK" and showed Moses His *goodness*. Take note! It was His goodness that changed Moses' countenance. This, the one time Moses' own countenance was changed, was only after a fresh revelation of God's goodness. Is this not what is missing in the New Testament Church? Is it possible that God intends to change the countenance of His people by a fresh revelation of His goodness? I think so. The world has seen a divided Church, an angry Church, a materialistic Church, and the list goes on. What would happen if they were to see a Church whose very countenance has been transformed by seeing Him, His glory—His goodness? This is what the world is crying for; they want to believe it's true—God is good. How we behold Him is what makes this a possibility.

DWELLING IN THE GLORY!

Another favorite story of mine also has to do with the glory of God. Ever since my dad taught us what it meant for us to be priests unto the Lord, ministering to Him with our thanksgiving, praise, and worship, I have embraced this as a primary purpose of my life. Every time I read in Scripture that there are people ministering to Him and then there's a response from Heaven, I get excited. The lessons are always profound, as there's

> Once you've tasted of the real reason that you're alive, nothing else will ever satisfy.

something of eternity on those moments. It doesn't matter whether it happened with David, Moses, or someone in the New Testament; those interactions are eternal in nature. And so it is with this next story.

> *It came even to pass, as the trumpeters and singers were as one, to make one sound to be heard in praising and thanking the Lord; and* **when they lifted up their voice** *with the trumpets and cymbals and instruments of music,* **and praised the Lord, saying, For he is good;** *for his mercy endureth for ever: that* **then the house was filled with a cloud,** *even the house of the Lord; so that the priests could not stand to minister by reason of the cloud: for* **the glory of the Lord had filled the house of God** *(2 Chronicles 5:13-14 KJV).*

Please note that the priests were offering the fruit of the lips (see Heb. 13:15) as their offering. While this happened in the Old Testament, it is clearly a New Testament practice, as the Law required the sacrifice of animals from the priests, not praise. Secondly, notice that the priests were in unity. Remember that the 120 believers in Acts chapters 1 and 2 were also in unity before the outpouring of the Holy Spirit took place. God once again put His glory upon a united people. (See Psalm 133.) God loves to manifest Himself upon His people when we're known for our love of each other. Thirdly, look at what they were praising God for—His goodness! They declared the Lord to be good! Once again we see a connection between the revelation of His goodness and His glory—His manifested presence. This is amazing, as the glory of God is to cover the earth as the waters cover the sea before time comes to an end (see Hab. 2:14). I suppose that many think this glory will become manifest through a military move of the return of the Messiah. His disciples thought that, too. (See Luke 19:11–17.) But I'd like to suggest that in the same way that the disciples were wrong about this, so we, too, are wrong, as we often fail to understand the process He loves to work through. He longs for our involvement in all these matters, not because He needs us. Co-laboring has been His heart from the beginning. And becoming a worshiping community that worships in spirit, in truth, and in unity will offer something to Him that He in turn will want to occupy—the praises of His people concerning His goodness.

> He was not ashamed to put His glory upon and in the physical buildings that people built in honor of His name. How much more will He put the glory in the house that He Himself builds?

I remember a number of years ago we had a prophetic song during one of our Sunday morning services. We call this type of song "the song of the Lord" in that it is a prophetic song, sung as though it were His voice singing over us as His people. It went something like this:

Did I not fill the tabernacle of Moses with My glory?

Did I not fill the temple of Solomon with My glory?

How much more should I fill the place that I build with My own hands?

My beloved, I am building you.

In that moment, we realized that God was referring to the Matthew 16:18 passage where Jesus said, *"I will build My church."* So here it is, a chance to catch a glimpse of where God puts His glory and why. He was not ashamed to put His glory upon and in the physical buildings that people built in honor of His name. How much more will He put the glory in the house that He Himself builds? And that house is the *Church*—the eternal dwelling place of God. (See Ephesians 2:22.) Obviously, I make no references to institutions or buildings when I say "Church." Those elements are good and useful tools of the actual Church. But they in themselves are not the Church. The Church is comprised of born-again believers who are as living stones, brought together into a spiritual house, to house a priesthood that will offer spiritual sacrifices, acceptable through Jesus. That is the revelation that Peter carried for us. (See 1 Peter 2:5.) I remind you that many consider Peter to be the foundation of the ministry of the Church. (See Matthew 16:18.) And to take it one step further, the glory that is put within that house is to manifest the goodness of God, or we miss the point altogether.

THE HOPE OF GLORY

The focus of the prophets, as well as the prophetic experiences contained throughout the Scriptures, oftentimes points to God's purposes for His people, the Church. The stories mentioned above reveal God's heart and plans for us. He has purposed to manifest Himself upon us and through us and, as a result, to transform the nature of the world around us. This must be seen, embraced, and received as a part of our *reason for being.*

The target of the Lord for us is still the glory. His glory is to become the dwelling place of God's people, as He in turn dwells in us. The apostle Paul used a phrase that is to grab our hearts: *"Christ in you, the hope of glory"* (Col. 1:27). Jesus Christ in us makes it possible to be restored fully to His purpose for us—living in the glory. If the glory of God contains the revelation of the goodness of God, then here is a key. Jesus Christ dwelling in us by the Holy Spirit is what makes the revelation of His goodness known to and through us to the world around us. And that is hope illustrated.

TRUSTING IN HIS GOODNESS

From my perspective, Psalm 27 is one of the most unusual and complete psalms in the Bible. It's a personal favorite. And as such, it has been a wonderful feeding place for my soul for many years. The writer illustrates his absolute trust in God (verses 1–3), the supreme value for His presence (verses 4–6), and his own devotion to obedience (verses 7–10). But the grand finale is the unveiling of His personal secret to strength (verses 11–14). He put it this way in verse 13: *"I would have despaired unless I had believed that I would see the goodness of the Lord in the land of the living."* It was his hope of seeing the goodness of God in his day that kept him from hopelessness.

Hopelessness is a thief, one that is often welcomed into Christian circles in the name of discernment. This deceptive influence must be marked and recognized as a tool of the enemy. If ever there was a season in all of history that the people of God need to *believe we'll see the glory of God*, it is now. God's people are to be known for their hope, regardless of circumstances, perhaps more than most any other virtue. As one of our own, Olivia Shupe, once observed, "The one with the most hope will always have the most influence." And we have good reason for it! God's goodness wreaks havoc on despair, depression, and hopelessness. Seeing His goodness releases the opportunity for faith. Expecting to taste and see His goodness keeps us impervious to the mental and emotional breakdowns that violate who He designed us to be—carriers of hope, and models of His goodness.

NOTE

1. "Legacy of Dr. George Washington Carver: Scientist Extraordinaire, Man of Faith, Educator and Humanitarian," accessed 6 June 2016, http://www.tuskegee.edu/about_us/ legacy_of_fame/george_w_carver.aspx.

Chapter Six

LOVE REQUIRES JUDGMENT

What I believe is so magnificent, so glorious, that it is beyond finite comprehension. To believe that the universe was created by a purposeful, benign Creator is one thing. To believe that this Creator took on human vesture, accepted death and mortality, was tempted, betrayed, broken, and all for love of us, defies reason. It is so wild that it terrifies some Christians who try to dogmatize their fear by lashing out at other Christians, because tidy Christianity with all answers given is easier than one which reaches out to the wild wonder of God's love, a love we don't even have to earn.

—MADELEINE L'ENGLE

If you take someone you love to the doctor to be examined because of a suspicious looking growth on his arm, you will want that doctor to bring judgment upon the growth and do whatever needs to be done to remove it. You'll not pick a doctor that shows mercy to the growth or one who becomes fascinated with how it is its own living entity. Only judgment is acceptable. I realize that sounds pretty silly at best to have a doctor who thinks like that, but I say it to make a point. There's no feeling of sympathy toward the tumor, nor is there any concern over what others might think. Judgment is the only acceptable response, as your love for that person requires such a reaction toward anything that threatens his well-being. Love requires that I fight for him by seeking for his protection. We live in a world where we celebrate judgments all the time. But for some reason, if the judgment comes from God, it's considered cruel and unloving. My friend Mike Bickle made a statement on this subject that really helped bring clarification for me in this issue: "All of God's judgments are aimed at whatever interferes with love." This is priceless, and so completely true.

If I had a neighbor that showed aggression and violence toward children, I would do whatever I could to inform the authorities and protect the children. While I tend to lean toward mercy for people who are caught up in sin, I would refuse to do anything that would protect their sinfulness, which would continue to threaten the safety of others. Such carelessness toward "friends" is not love at all. Love stands for something. It is honest and confrontational when necessary. For example, it is not love to see someone you care for in a burning building and leave her there no matter how sincere she is, or how good of a person she is, or how rough her childhood was. Love requires action. Love requires judgment—"This building is on fire. Get out or you will die!" Love chooses the best. Love doesn't choose what simply feels good to us.

Let's take the subject of God's judgment a step further. First, let's recognize that if God were hell-bent on bringing condemnation on all mankind, He could and would have accomplished that a long time ago by simply declaring the word needed to bring it about. The whole point of this book is that condemnation is not in His heart. As stated earlier, *"God takes no pleasure in the death of the wicked"* (Ezek. 18:23). Yet the fact remains, judgment has to happen because God is holy—He is perfect in beauty, with undefiled purity, completely separate from all that is dark and evil and totally driven by love in all actions, thoughts, and intentions. Sin violates and contaminates all that He has made, creating a breach between Creator and creation. Yet judgment had to be released because He is love. Out of necessity He declared, *"The soul that sins shall die"* (Ezek. 18:20). That was something that came forth because He is love. Please notice that statement is in the same chapter as *"God takes no pleasure in the death of the wicked"* (Ezek. 18:23).

God cannot lie—it would be an impossible violation of His nature and being. But the most amazing thing happened. God chose to pour out the much-needed judgment upon His Son, Jesus, instead of us. Because of His great love for us, Jesus volunteered to take our place in bearing the penalty of death that each of us deserved. In doing so, He satisfied the appetite of the Law for our judgment. And if that weren't enough, He then qualified us to receive the inheritance that only Jesus deserved. I remind you that He alone is the One who lived without sin, blemish, or compromise of any kind. In all honesty, I would have been totally satisfied to have my appointment with hell cancelled. But for the Father to qualify me for the same reward as Jesus? That is as far beyond my grasp as any thought or idea could possibly be.

ROCK THE BOAT!

Love requires judgment if it's to be real love. Love without judgment is apathetic, lethargic, and passionless; it really isn't love at all. Any belief system that promotes conviction without emotional expression is more consistent with Buddhism than it is with the Gospel of Jesus Christ. It doesn't rock the boat. That is something that Jesus had no problem doing time and time again. Jesus was far from passive. The position of "not rocking the boat" is often applauded as peaceful, when in reality it's a peace that can only exist where the *person of peace* controls the circumstances or setting. Jesus is the authentic Person of Peace (Prince of Peace) who demonstrates what real peace looks like. He did this while being accused, persecuted, beaten, and crucified. Circumstances don't control, influence, or determine the reign of such peace, as it is superior in every possible way. It is anchored in a person who changes not.

> **Love requires judgment if it's to be real love. Love without judgment is apathetic, lethargic, and passionless; it really isn't love at all.**

Love is a person—God is love. He loves people to the point of sacrificing the life of His own Son on a cross. That zeal is beyond our ability to measure, and yet we're alive because of it.

UNIVERSALISM? NO!

Many who have started to catch a glimpse of God's goodness have followed their own logic and reason far outside of biblical parameters. That is always a danger. We all have convictions and ideas about what is true. I'm referring now to someone in the process of growing and developing in Christ, not the person given to a spirit of deception. As someone once said, we don't know what we don't know. But we must not try to make the Scriptures say what we believe; we must adjust what we believe according to the mandates given in Scripture. The Word of God cuts and prunes our original ideas into a truly biblical shape until they represent Jesus well. Let me illustrate: If I see where the Scripture says, *"There is no fear in love"* (1 John 4:18) and on top of that, "God loves us" (see John 3:16), and I conclude that there is no fear of God in the New Testament, I have based my conclusion on the logic of two Scriptures and two very powerful principles. But is it accurate? It could seem so to some. But this is where we need the whole of Scripture to shape and enliven what we think and teach. The apostle Paul said, *"Therefore, having these promises, beloved, let us cleanse ourselves from all defilement of flesh and spirit, perfecting holiness in the fear of God"* (2 Cor. 7:1). What do I do now? This is obvious instruction given to those who follow Jesus Christ as their Lord and Savior. At this point, far too many try to change what the Scripture says to protect their definition or what they feel they've been learning. It is wiser to hold in tension two contradictory ideas than it is to twist what the Scripture has said, discounting the one that doesn't fit your ideal. (More on that later in the chapter entitled "The Importance of Mystery.") Everything must yield to the Word of God.

There's even danger from many in recent days to criticize Paul or Peter (or whoever has written the Scripture in question) and attribute what the writer said to his own biases. The thought is that Scripture contains teachings that are inconsistent with the teachings of Jesus. That approach scares me big time. That means the person who is critiquing what the Scripture writer has said actually has an opinion that has greater value and authority than what the Bible itself says. The Word of God then becomes pointless in that it becomes subject to the opinions of others. It's so much easier to believe God, trust God, and ask the Holy Spirit to lead us into all truth. So when I read that there is the fear of the Lord in the New Testament, I have to adjust my definition. What I think, live, and teach must be consistent with the Bible, so I allow what is written to prune my definition until it will stand the test of God's Word itself.

Forgiveness of sin is a primary focus of the New Testament message. This is a most incredible gift—we are forgiven. But part two of this gift is that our nature to sin is changed. But the part that once again changes the landscape of life on planet Earth is that every person who is in Christ becomes the righteousness of Christ (see 2 Cor. 5:21). No wonder the psalmist stated this principle of forgiveness in the most profound way: *"But there is forgiveness with You, that You may be feared"* (Ps. 130:4). That has to be one of the most unnatural combinations of truths in the Bible. He *forgives* us, and because of that, we *fear* Him. As you can imagine, this kind of fear does not drive people from Him, instead it draws people to Him.

Here's another example of pruning our theology. Some would say that because God loves people, and it is not His desire to see the death of the wicked, people don't go to hell. That is a popular reasoning of the day we live in. It is true that hell was created for the devil and his demons, and not for people (see Matt. 25:41). But Jesus talks a lot about hell, outer darkness, weeping, and gnashing of teeth. It takes a lot of work to make the Bible say there is no hell for people and even more work to say everybody goes to Heaven. This concept of Universalism is from hell itself, as it strips the Church of any sense of urgency and accountability for embracing the Great Commission. If Universalism were true, there would be little need for the bulk of Scripture, as it becomes pointless in a world where all roads lead to the same place. Once again, the Bible must be used to shape our thoughts and opinions, even when those Scriptures seem to defy logic and reason. Absolute trust in God, His nature, and His Word is the beginning place of this journey. It is from that place of trust we discover Him, the One who is superior in all logic and reason. I think it can be said that many will miss out on the discovery of God's nature because they lack the trust necessary to enter into that experience. True trust outweighs all the questions we may have.

LOVING PEOPLE AT THEIR WORST

Standing with people in the midst of their problems seems to be a fading value. To stand with someone who is in sin is frowned upon, as it makes others think we support their sin. Jesus sure seemed to have a different approach and was called a friend of sinners as a result. On a practical side, it serves no purpose to create an atmosphere that encourages people to freely exhibit their sinfulness without consequences. It's much wiser to stand with someone with issues *if* he wants to clean up his mess. Choices have consequences, good and bad. That is life. Our loyalty to one another must be solid, but it must not empower others toward wrongdoing. But as crazy as it sounds, unsanctified mercy has taken the place of true mercy. Unsanctified mercy empowers people toward sin without an awareness of consequences. True mercy is shown to people in trouble by loving them when they don't deserve it, but also by telling them the truth, working to bring them into a freedom that God intended for everyone. True freedom is not doing as we please. It's being enabled to do the right thing well.

> **We are the most useless in our faith when our confidence for transformation depends on the return of Christ instead of the work of Christ. His return will be glorious! But His work set the stage for a transformed people to transform the nature of the world they live in.**

THE LAST DAYS

There are many promises concerning the last days. Truth be told, we have been living in the last days for two thousand years. The prophet Joel spoke of the outpouring of the Holy Spirit in Acts 2 as that which would take place *"in the last days"* (Joel 2:28–29). So if those were the last days, we are certainly in the last of the last days.

Jesus had much to say about the days we live in. For example, He said we would be hearing of *"wars and rumors of wars...for nation will rise up against nation...and in various places there will be famines and earthquakes"* (Matt. 24:6–7). It's important to note that Jesus wasn't giving His people a promise. In other words, this was not a word that the Church was to exercise their faith over to bring about what God had purposed. Instead, Jesus is simply describing the conditions into which He was sending His last days' army with transformational influence.

Everyone's *last days theology* requires faith. For some, it is a faith to endure until we're rescued. For others, it's a faith to obtain in response to our commission. I'll take the latter. We are the most useless in our faith when our confidence for transformation depends on the return of Christ instead of the work of Christ. His return will be glorious! But His work set the stage for a transformed people to transform the nature of the world they live in. It is a glorious work, being done by a glorious bride that the Glorious One will return for.

There are many things recorded throughout Scripture that go far beyond information. They are promises—something we are to believe God for. To keep the subject of promises in perspective, I remind you that Israel was given a promise of entering the Promised Land. Yet the generation that first heard that promise didn't enter it. Did God let them down? After all, it was God who gave them the promise. No. They had responsibilities in bringing about God's fulfilled promise. They became hard-hearted and tested God over and over again until God said "no" to their entering His promise to them. My friend Larry Randolph describes this issue best. He states, "While God will always fulfill His promises, He is not obligated to fulfill our potential." Some promises are given to us from God. They reveal His heart, His desire, and His purpose for us. But it's quite possible they may never happen. Why? Because they must be believed and acted upon before they become a reality for us. There is a role that we play in most of what God has declared over us. To blame God is simply irresponsible.

There are so many promises from God concerning the days that we live in, but many of us are blind to them. The typical response is if it's a good promise with blessings attached, it's for the Millennium. If there are trials, tribulations, and the like, it's for now. I think the main reason we become blind to these promises is that we are accustomed to being opposed, and we've definitely seen evil increase. That then becomes the standard by which we interpret what is coming our way. It isn't. We do not have an inferior gospel. God gave us surpassingly great promises to help us navigate well during challenging days and circumstances.

When God gives us a promise, it's as though He has gone into our future and brought back the word needed to get us to where He wants us to be.

There is an unusual parallel with what the Church is experiencing and the story of Israel going into the Promised Land. It is sometimes frighteningly similar. It's as though God said, "The whole Promised Land belongs to you, but you'll inherit it little by little. If you get it too quickly, you won't be able to manage what you'll inherit, and it will turn around and bite you. Embrace the process, for in doing so I am making you capable of keeping what

I give you, if you'll simply obey from the heart." Admittedly, that may be an overly simplistic paraphrase, but you get the point. God is working to make us capable of surviving His blessings.

NOTABLE PROMISES

When God gives us a promise, it's as though He has gone into our future and brought back the word needed to get us to where He wants us to be. And so it is with these two brilliant promises of God for His people of the last days.

> *Afterward the children of Israel shall return and **seek the Lord** their God and David their king. **They shall fear the Lord** and **His goodness** in the **latter days*** (Hosea 3:5).

Notice that there is a connection between seeking God, God's goodness, and people fearing Him, with the last days as the setting for the fulfillment of this promise. I suggest we use our faith to believe for what was promised here.

> *Then it shall be to Me a name of joy, a praise, and an honor before all nations of the earth, **who shall hear all the good that I do** to them; **they shall fear** and tremble **for all the goodness** and all the prosperity that **I provide** for it* (Jeremiah 33:9).

Here are two startling promises given by God. I don't remember ever hearing a preacher who specialized in the last days talking about these passages, nor even the subjects they address. The promise is clear—God's goodness will be seen upon His people. Consider this: It just might be that the most overlooked evangelistic tool of the Church is the blessing of the Lord upon our lives. We've seen blessings abused, materialistic kingdoms built in His name, and other self-centered expressions. But when we react to the errors of others, we are prone to create yet another error.

The Bible says that others will see His goodness and will in turn fear the Lord. I wonder, how good does that goodness have to be for people to see it and actually tremble? It's hard to imagine His goodness in a casual or incidental manner bringing about that response. It would have to be so clear, and in my opinion so *extreme*, so as to be obviously manifested from God Himself, that people tremble with fear.

Put on your seat belts! We're about to enter the journey of a lifetime. It's a time where opposition increases, the need for our help becomes more obvious, and the blessing of God separates us from others. Knowing how to steward such things is paramount to our fulfilling His heart to disciple nations.

PSALM 67[1]

An Invocation and a Doxology

> *To the Chief Musician. On Stringed Instruments.*
> *A Psalm. A Song.*
> *God be merciful to us and bless us,*
> *And cause His face to shine upon us. Selah.*
> *That Your way may be known on earth,*
> ***Your salvation among all nations.***
> *Let the peoples praise You, O God;*
> *Let all the peoples praise You.*
> *Oh, let the nations be glad and sing for joy!*
> *For You shall judge the people righteously,*
> *And govern the nations on earth. Selah.*

Let the peoples praise You, O God;
Let all the peoples praise You.
Then the earth shall yield her increase;
God, our own God, shall bless us.
God shall bless us,
And all the ends of the earth shall fear Him
(Psalm 67).

You'll notice that I highlighted two parts of this psalm. The first one says, *"Your salvation among all nations"* (Ps. 67:2). And the second one is, *"And all the ends of the earth shall fear Him"* (Ps. 67:7). Both statements are evangelistic in nature, talking about nations coming to Christ. This is astonishing and is consistent with the heart of God revealed in the Great Commission to *disciple nations.* (See Matthew 28:19.) But the question that must be asked is, what brought about the conversion of nations in this prophetic psalm? The conclusion is they feared God and experienced His salvation! But what caused them to see the heart of God and His nature to the point that they were convicted of their own sins and turned in repentance to Him? What caused such a miraculous turn of events? Blessings. Blessings are what preceded both statements of nations coming to Christ—*bless us so they know what You're like,* and *God shall bless us, and they'll come to Him* (my paraphrase).

Favor upon me must benefit the people under my influence, or it is misused.

No wonder the devil works so hard to undermine our confidence in His absolute goodness. It's that specific revelation that is key to a massive last days' revival, where there is a harvest of entire nations. The stakes have never been higher. Settling into the realm of His goodness has never been more necessary than it is now.

But there is a challenge with blessings. No generation that I'm aware of has been able to navigate a life full of blessing while still serving God sacrificially. Blessings create entitlement, superiority, independence, materialism, greed, and on and on. The problem isn't with the blessing of God. It's us. I believe God would provide for us beyond any of our wildest dreams. And while I don't want to make this term *blessings* about money alone, it must include it. But what would that blessing do to us? Many people only have a prayer life because they have troubles. Who then would pray? Many develop community because their personal needs are so deep that they need others to make it through their week. What happens when that need is not quite so obvious? Raising up a generation that can live with blessing while still bearing their cross is the challenge of the day. From my perspective, God disciplines us so that His blessings don't kill us. It's really true.

Blessings are manifestations of increased favor. Yet favor has a purpose. Without discovering that purpose, we are prone to self-promotion and personal kingdom building. The queen of Sheba put it this way when she acknowledged the favor that rested upon Solomon. *"Blessed be the Lord your God who delighted in you to set you on the throne of Israel;* **because the Lord loved Israel** *forever, therefore* **He made you king***, to do justice and righteousness"* (1 Kings 10:9). There it is. Because God loved Israel, He showed favor upon Solomon and made him king. Favor was to benefit those He served as king or it would be misused. It basically comes down to this: Favor upon me must benefit the people under my influence, or it is misused.

We are coming into increased times of favor and blessing, with greater and greater areas of responsibility. I'm not saying we're coming into a life of ease and self-exalting bounty. It's just that He is making it more and more obvious who carries His heart by releasing an increased favor upon them for influence. That is that mark of His blessing.

Our positions of increase are unto something. The problems that our cities and nations are facing have no answers outside of God. We, the people of unfailing hope, have the opportunity to serve and serve well, bringing the King and His Kingdom into the everyday lives of people all around us. He is putting something upon us that will help them to see Him. If I use that which God is placing into my charge for personal gain, I will find myself seriously disappointed. But if I can live with His favor and blessing and use it for its intended purpose, nations will turn to Christ. That is His promise. That is His Word. And it is so, because He is good.

NOTE

1. I wrote much more extensively on Psalm 67 in my book *The Power that Changes the World.* I strongly encourage you to read it, as I believe it provides a prophetic template for what God intends to do in these days that we now live in.

Chapter Seven

WE HAVE A FATHER

You must make your choice. Either this man was, and is, the Son of God, or else a madman or something worse. You can shut him up for a fool, you can spit at him and kill him as a demon or you can fall at his feet and call him Lord and God, but let us not come with any patronizing nonsense about his being a great human teacher. He has not left that open to us. He did not intend to.

—C.S. LEWIS, *Mere Christianity*

Why did Jesus become a man and come to earth? I realize that is a rather simple question understood by believers and sometimes by nonbelievers as well. Yet I wanted to find statements from Scripture answering this question. So years ago, I set out to read the New Testament in its entirety, looking for the answer to that one question—why did Jesus, the eternal Son of God, come to earth and become a man? Although I have misplaced the list derived from that study, here are a few of the passages and statements. We know:

1. Jesus came to atone for our sins. (See 1 John 2:2; 3:5.)

2. He came to take upon Himself the punishment that we deserved—our punishment in death. He then made it possible for us to receive what only He deserved—eternal life. (See Romans 5:6–11.)

3. He came to destroy the works of the evil one. (See 1 John 3:8.)

4. He came to make an open display of the foolishness of the devil and reveal the wisdom of the cross. (See Colossians 2:15.)

5. He came that we might have abundant life. (See John 10:10.)

6. He came to initiate the present-tense awareness of the Kingdom of God—the realm and effects of God's rule. (See Matthew 6:10.)

7. Jesus came to save men's lives, not destroy them. (See Luke 9:56.)

This is not at all a comprehensive list. But it is enough to illustrate my point. I had studied this subject from cover to cover, yet I missed the primary reason for His coming. *Jesus came to reveal the Father.* Every point I had on my list was actually a sub-point to the primary reason. Jesus came to a planet of orphans to reveal what we needed most—the Father. Tragically, that wonderful revelation suffers under the broken condition of our present family culture. Because so many have suffered under the abuse or neglect of their biological fathers, the wonder of this phenomenon is often lost. On the other hand, there's never been a moment more ripe for this greatest answer to human brokenness and need. Most of the ills of humanity would be healed with that one revelation—Jesus came to set our focus, attention, and affection on the Father, who is good. Our Father really is perfect goodness.

It wasn't that the goodness of God was missing in the Old Testament. In fact, that revelation of His goodness starts there: *"The Lord is good"* (Nah. 1:7). That revelation is laced throughout the Old Testament with His continual display of mercy toward a rebellious people. Time and time again, Israel brought disaster upon themselves through worshiping idols made by hands and giving themselves over to the sexual sins of the surrounding nations. Yet when they cried out to Him, He delivered them without complaint or punishment. His goodness drips from page after page of Scripture. Yet for some it gets lost in the midst of the wars, judgments, diseases, and disasters. When Jesus came, He made it nearly impossible to forget the new standard, as He brought a face to that goodness. It became personified in Him. Goodness became measurable—taste worthy. (See Psalm 34:8.)

> **Jesus came to a planet of orphans to reveal what we needed most—the Father.**

Both the mystery and the revelation of God's goodness are contained in Jesus. In reading through the Gospel of John, the Gospel that contains the bulk of the revelation of why Jesus came to earth, we find out that when we see Jesus, we see the Father. (See John 14:9.) We then discover that He says only what the Father is saying. (See John 12:49–50.) We also come to realize that Jesus does only what the Father is doing. (See John 5:19.) And so everything that we love and admire about Jesus is actually a precise and calculated manifestation of the Father. God is *the* Father, and the Father is good.

Throughout our history God has spoken to our ancestors by His prophets in many different ways. The revelation he gave them was only a fragment at a time, building one truth upon another. But to us living in these last days, God now speaks to us openly in the language of a Son, the appointed Heir of everything, for through him God created the panorama of all things and all time.

The Son is the dazzling radiance of God's splendor, the exact expression of God's true nature—his mirror image!
(Hebrews 1:1–3a, TPT)

This is a stunning section of Scripture. It tells us that Jesus is the exact representation of the Father—His nature and His person. He is that which emanates from the Father's being, manifesting His glory (remember goodness, Exodus 33:18–19). It's interesting to note that when Jesus informed the disciples that He was going back to the Father, but that He would send the Comforter (the Holy Spirit), He used a very specific word. *"I will ask the Father, and He will give you another Helper, that He may be with you forever"* (John 14:16). The word used here for "another" means *one that is exactly the same.* Let me illustrate. As I write this book, I'm looking at the furniture in my living room. There are two couches facing each other in front of a fireplace. They are exactly the same—mirror images of each other. We have another couch in our family room, but its color, shape, and size are quite a bit different from the two in our living room. I could accurately say, "I have *another* couch in my family room." But I couldn't use the word used in John 14 because, while my family room couch qualifies as a couch, it isn't exactly the same as the two in my living room. What's the point? When we look at Jesus, He is *exactly* the same as His Father. Then Jesus sent the Holy Spirit, who is *exactly* like Jesus. In other words, God wanted to make sure that there would be no chance of missing the revelation needed to permeate and shift the course of history at this point and time—the revelation of our God as a good and perfect Father.

Jesus reveals a Father who is not abusive or self-serving. The Holy Spirit, who now lives in us, reaffirms the wonder and beauty of this perfectly good Father. The work that He is doing in us is all about deepening our connection to the Father, who brings identity, purpose, destiny, and an awareness of unlimited resources to accomplish our purpose in life. When the Holy Spirit is able to do His perfect work in us, our connection to all that is good is strengthened and made clear. This revelation of God as our Father is the ultimate expression of the goodness of God.

THE BEAUTY OF DISCIPLINE

When I talk about this perfect Father, I'm not talking about someone who refuses to discipline His children. And while the subject of discipline is not what people want to hear, it is real and needed. The truth of the matter is that He loves us too much to leave us as we are. Some of the most significant changes only take place in that context. According to Scripture, discipline proves we belong to Him as sons and daughters. (See Hebrews 12:7–8.) Those who are without discipline are not real heirs and descendants. They are fakes. They may talk the talk, but you can't authentically walk the walk without discipline.

When Beni and I were raising our children, we determined to make discipline an event, not an impulsive outburst. Outbursts are for the sake of the parent, not the child. "That child crossed my will, and I'll show him who is boss." And so the physically larger person yells or gives a swat. In a strange way, it makes the parent feel vindicated, and that he or she is at least trying to keep that child from becoming an uncontrollable detriment to society. We all want to be good caregivers to our children.

Beni and I purposed to never discipline our children out of anger. Outbursts and anger had nothing to do with a loving concern for a child. Giving a swat on the butt or a verbal outburst does little to shape a child's heart in the right way. Impulsive reactions undermine our intent. Discipline then becomes a release valve for the parent and has little to do with the well-being or the forming of the child's heart. Changing the focus changes the method, which changes the outcome.

Our policy was, before there was discipline of any kind, I sent the child to his or her room so that I could take whatever time needed to prepare my heart. I had to make sure I was going in the room for the child's sake, and not mine. I had to be firm, but not angry; compassionate, but not careless. Interestingly, the child that was disciplined usually wanted to spend the rest of the evening with me, on my lap, or playing a game with me. Done correctly, discipline serves and, strangely, unites. It doesn't divide.

Jesus talked about this in John 15. This is the chapter on the vine, the vinedresser, and the fruit. To illustrate discipline, Jesus talks about pruning. God rewards all growth with pruning. It doesn't happen only when there's something wrong. It's that, left untended, vines will grow to a place where they bear little to no fruit. All the energy of the vine goes into growing branches and leaves. God is very concerned with fruit from our lives and does whatever is needed to keep that priority in place. If we are left unchecked, our growth is in appearance (religious—form without power). And just as Adam and Eve covered themselves with leaves to hide their nakedness, so we hide our immaturity behind the appearance of growth and not in the substance of Christ-likeness.

There is to be fruit of being like Jesus—converts, miracles, answers to prayer, and a changed life.

> *I am the true vine, and My Father is the vinedresser. Every branch in Me that does not bear fruit, He takes away; and every branch that bears fruit, He prunes it so that it may bear more fruit. You are already clean because of the word which I have spoken to you* (John 15:1–3).

I find this passage very interesting. Jesus lets them know there will be pruning in their lives. But He follows the statement with *"You are already clean because of the word which I have spoken to you."* The word for *clean* is the same basic word as *prune*. And our becoming clean (disciplined) in this context happens through His Word/His voice. Think about it—pruning/discipline takes place when He talks to us. That is amazing. I grew up thinking that bad circumstances in my life were His discipline. That is inconsistent with the lesson given by Jesus to His disciples. Since then I've learned that oftentimes the bad circumstances are brought on by us, but they serve to turn us back to a place of listening. The large fish that swallowed Jonah wasn't the discipline of the Lord. He ran into that "wall" running from God (the voice). But the fish helped to bring Jonah back to the place of wanting to hear from God. I'm not saying that circumstances can never be a part of discipline. I'm just saying that even then, He simply wants to talk to us to bring about the change in us that is needed. A lot happens when He talks and we listen from the heart, thus becoming the doers of His Word as He always intended. (See James 1:21.)

JESUS DISCIPLINES HIS DISCIPLES

Luke chapter 9 is one of the more interesting and entertaining chapters in the Bible. It's worthy of great study. This chapter is my favorite in seeing how Jesus dealt with His disciples when they were doing and saying stupid things. Jesus had made these guys very powerful, and now they are doing things that are very inconsistent with the standard that Jesus set for Himself and for them.

This is the chapter where the twelve are given power and authority to minister in Jesus' name (verse 2) and are then sent out in pairs to their hometowns to preach the Gospel of the Kingdom (see Luke 9:6). When they return, they meet with Jesus to let Him know what they said and did. There is obvious excitement, as they did what Jesus did without Him being there. Miracles took place through their words and hands. Jesus later let them know that their real celebration had to be in the fact their names are written in Heaven (see Luke 10:20). Following their time of great ministry success, strange things began to surface. The first was they began to argue as to who was the greatest. I can only imagine that they began to think this way because of the miracles that flowed through them. Remember, they were sent out two by two, which means there were ten other disciples who were not present when the powerful things happened through them. In their minds, it might have been hard for them to imagine that the other disciples experienced things that were quite as significant as what they experienced. Jesus, knowing what they were talking about, realized it was time to *prune a branch*. If their concept of greatness was based on the miracles that flowed through them, they were in trouble. If that *branch* were allowed to grow, it would remove all possibility of lasting fruit for the glory of God. And so Jesus pointed to a child, and let them know what real greatness in the Kingdom looked like. He said, *"or the one who is least among all of you, this is the one who is great"* (Luke 9:48b). Jesus introduced them once again to the mystery of His Kingdom, where we gain by giving and rise by going low.

As soon as Jesus addressed their preoccupation with personal greatness, the disciples made another blunder. They saw someone trying to cast out demons in Jesus' name. So they rebuked him, trying to maintain their franchise on Kingdom power. It's almost like they're saying, "OK. We get it. We're not better than each other. But we are certainly better than him!" Because they had the access to Jesus that no one else had, they took that on as a measure of personal accomplishment, instead of personal responsibility, as in *"to whom much is given, much is required"* (Luke 12:48). They missed it. Once again Jesus spoke to them life-changing words: *"Do not hinder him; for he who is not against you is for you"* (Luke 9:50). I remind you, Jesus brings discipline to the twelve, pruning back a branch that would not bear fruit in the future if it continued to develop in the direction it was going. The idea of elitism would cost them greatly in the future if it was not addressed now. They also needed to know that some of their support would come from people who are not in their club. As stated in John 15:3, this process of His word spoken to them is what is making them clean/pruned. Issues of the heart are always addressed when Jesus talks. Receiving that word changes us. (See James 1:21.)

That was not the end. The problems of their hearts seemed only to increase and rise to the surface in the most inopportune times. Remember, this chapter is the record of the great experiment— giving power to very imperfect disciples. In the very next scene, James and John want to call down fire upon an entire city because they rejected their ministry. The spirit of murder is now functioning through the disciples to the point that they actually want to kill the citizens of an entire city. Obviously, the heart to murder is wrong.

But the need to be vindicated in order to feel good about ourselves is a very shaky ground to build upon. This branch (thought, belief, and idea) had to be dealt with through discipline.

As a side note, what kinds of things did they see God do through their ministries on their recent missionary journey that would make them think that with Jesus' approval they could actually pull this off—call down fire from Heaven? If this branch were allowed to grow, it could threaten the very purpose of the vine entirely. Jesus exposes their hearts with a word: *"You do not know what kind of spirit you are of; for the Son of Man did not come to destroy men's lives, but to save them"* (Luke 9:55–56). The New King James Version of this story emphasizes that they used Elijah as an example for what

> The Day of Judgment is in His hands. The day of mercy is in ours.

they were asking. *"Lord, do You want us to command fire to come down from heaven and consume them, just as Elijah did?"* (Luke 9:54). I think it's funny how often we find a verse to justify what we know in our hearts to be wrong. The disciples had already witnessed Jesus' approach to people and knew that His heart was one of great compassion and mercy. It's also interesting to note that to call down fire was perfect in Elijah's day but was now very wrong in Jesus' day. Elijah perfectly fulfilled his assignment. But his assignment wasn't to reveal the Father. Jesus, knowing that such an action would undermine the revelation of the Father, told His disciples that they would have to be empowered by a different spirit to carry out that plan of calling down fire upon a city. He then listed another reason for His coming—*to save men's lives, not destroy them.* I wish more people would get this. I once had a lady curse and rebuke me and actually try to cast a demon out of me at the back door of the sanctuary for not agreeing with her in prayer for the destruction of San

Francisco. Thankfully the only devil present left when she did. I had her kindly escorted to the exit.

Don't get me wrong, the sins of that city, and most others, are great. Inexcusable? Yes. Unforgiveable? No. This isn't the Day of Judgment. This is the day of great mercy. The Day of Judgment is in His hands. The day of mercy is in ours. All of us who received His forgiveness have done so because of His mercy. All we're praying is, "God, I know I'm no better than the people of this city. Please show them the same undeserved mercy You've shown to me." God longs to extend His mercy to people who no longer recognize the difference between their right hand and their left. (See Jonah 4:11.) That is not a derogatory remark about their intelligence. Far from it. It's a statement about the ability of the majority to distinguish between right and wrong. This is a day when insanity is called sanity, wrong is considered right, and foolishness is called nobility. Babies are murdered in the name of *rights*, while animals are protected in the name of *responsibilities*. And all this is fought for with an *offering* of zeal that God alone is worthy of receiving. We are in desperate need of His mercy upon our cities and nations.

Luke 9 records the great experiment in which Jesus entrusts His power and authority to twelve men who really aren't that stable or mature. The very fact that they would argue about who is the greatest, and want to restrict the activities of all who don't belong to their group, and then follow it up with attempted murder should let us know the condition of these men. I can assure you, if I had one of my pastoral staff members confide in me that he was asked to leave a city because his ministry was rejected, and now he had a plan to blow up the entire community, I would be greatly concerned about his place in ministry. I'd at least restrict his activities and have him get help. Jesus doesn't even seem surprised when these issues come up. And in every case, He has a specific word of correction and redirection. But nowhere does He lose His temper. Nowhere does He punish them and make them "sit on the bench" while the others continue following Him. He spoke, and they were changed. And these issues never came up again.

THE FUNNIEST SURPRISE OF ALL!

Many would consider entrusting authority and power to the twelve disciples to be a failed experiment. Apparently Jesus doesn't, as He then does the unexplainable—He follows this experiment by entrusting this same power and authority to seventy others, releasing them into the same kind of ministry as the twelve. *"Now after this the Lord appointed seventy others, and sent them in pairs ahead of Him to every city and place where He Himself was going to come"* (Luke 10:1). That is astonishing. Apparently, Jesus is not as afraid of messes as we are. One of my favorite ministry verses in the Bible is in Proverbs 14:4: *"Where no oxen are, the manger is clean, but much revenue comes by the strength of the ox."* The goal of many in ministry is no messes. And that becomes the measure of success. I remind you, graveyards are orderly and clean. Nurseries filled with babies are not. One is alive, and the other is dead. If you want increase, get a shovel, and learn how to patiently work with people who are in process.

> **Graveyards are orderly and clean. Nurseries filled with babies are not. One is alive, and the other is dead. If you want increase, get a shovel, and learn how to patiently work with people who are in process.**

Jesus reveals the Father as perfectly good. He revealed Him in every word (teaching) and action (miracles and acts of kindness). He then gives us the Holy Spirit to emulate Him through us. There's to be no mistake or let down in the ongoing revelation of what the Father is like. It is to happen through us as it happened through Jesus.

SECRETS TO SAVING SIN-FILLED CITIES

Many want to curse sinners, but that curse is a misuse of authority and purpose. God calls us priests of the Lord (see 1 Pet. 2:9). In priestly ministry, we represent people before God and God before people. Representing people before God is a prayer-type ministry, often called intercession. The task at hand is to stand in the gap (the place of obvious breakdown in spiritual equilibrium and values) and pray for mercy on their behalf. (See Ezekiel 22:30.) Someone did that for us. We must now do it for others. Tragically, in the Ezekiel passage mentioned, God couldn't find anyone who would cry out for mercy for those in need. To take our God-given assignment to pray on behalf of someone and turn that moment into a curse is a complete misuse of a God-given responsibility. Giving an account to God for the misuse of that assignment is going to sting. This might be part of the reason why the Bible says that He will wipe away our tears.

God longs for us to co-labor with Him. Intercessory prayer is such a role. And so is the lifestyle of miracles. Jesus brought a rebuke to three cities because they had seen His ongoing life of miracles (see Matt. 11:20–24). While they applauded His works, they didn't adjust their lifestyle to this standard that was now being revealed to them. In other words, they didn't repent. *To repent* basically means "to change our way of thinking." So the miracles they saw didn't change how they thought or how they saw their responsibilities in life. Jesus then made a shocking conclusion: *"If the miracles had occurred in Sodom which occurred in you, it would have remained to this day"* (Matt. 11:23). Do you see it? If a ministry like Jesus' ministry were to have happened in the city of Sodom, the city known by the judgment of God released over it, it would still be here. Sodom would have repented! Miracles, in the measure that Jesus demonstrated, will turn a *Sodom* from a city of judgment to a city of purpose with great legacy and endurance. Their lostness makes purpose and destiny easy to recognize. Religious cities, in the sense of form without power, are insulated from realizing their need for God and the direction He brings.

God longs to show mercy. But when people partner with one another to curse a city, or a celebrity, a politician, an evil boss, we are violating the reason we're alive. He looks for those who will stand in the gap with intercession. Why? Because He is good! And without people standing in the gap, interceding for those needing mercy, the manifestation of His goodness will be missed.

THIS CHANGES EVERYTHING

Everything He said and did worked to fulfill that one assignment—reveal the Father. When I realized that simple point, it changed everything. It created a context and, more importantly, a reason for every word and action of Jesus. The Father was to be made known to this planet of orphans.

When Jesus responded to the cry of blind Bartimaeus, He was representing the Father. There's not one of us, if we had the ability to turn our blind child into a seeing child, that wouldn't do it. It's what fathers do. We fix things. And in this case, Jesus took care of his blindness by opening his eyes, but he also gave him a new identity. The blind man threw aside his beggar's garment when he came to Jesus. That garment was his badge of employment, given by the priests, to prove he was deserving of alms.

When they brought the woman caught in adultery to Jesus to see what He would do, He once again represented the Father. The religious leaders brought stones to kill her according to the Law they lived under. But Jesus came with a different assignment. He bent over and wrote in the dirt, telling those intending to stone her to go ahead, under this condition: *"the one without sin cast the first stone"* (John 8:7). Interestingly, the only one without sin refused to cast a stone at all. Instead, He revealed the Father. In reality, this was a Father/daughter moment.

All those intending to stone her to death fled the scene. Whatever He wrote released such an atmosphere of grace that those driven by judgment had to leave. Jesus then did what any one of us would have done if our daughter were lost in such moral failure and humiliating shame. He served her. Jesus didn't care what the religious leaders thought of Him. The opinions of the crowd didn't matter either. The Father had to be seen. And more importantly, the Father had to be known by this one who was lost, this one who was manifesting her orphaned heart.

In the Old Covenant she would have been stoned to death. But this is a different season, even though the Old Covenant was still in play, as the blood of Jesus had not been shed yet. Her sin wasn't ignored or treated lightly. Once she acknowledged that her accusers had left and there was now no one to condemn her, Jesus said, *"Neither do I condemn you. Go and sin no more"* (John 8:11). He disciplined her—with loving words.

Every action and every word pointed to a perfect Father, one who is completely good. When the disciples thought children were not quite as important as the adults Jesus was ministering to, Jesus corrected them. Children flock around good dads. On top of that, parents entrust their children to good dads. Jesus simply illustrated this phenomenon that took the disciples a while to catch on to.

He was manifesting the Father to people, and the children saw it before most.

> And they were bringing children to Him so that He might touch them; but the disciples rebuked them. But when Jesus saw this, He was indignant and said to them, "Permit the children to come to Me; do not hinder them; for the kingdom of God belongs to such as these" (Mark 10:13–14).

Page after page and story after story shows how Jesus revealed the Father in word and deed. The priestly prayer of Jesus in John 17 opens for us some of the most intimate moments between Jesus and His Father. To me it sounds like Jesus is giving an account of how He spent His time on planet Earth to His Father. The entire chapter is worth reading just for this single purpose—how did Jesus give an account of His life on earth? Just seeing this helps us to see the understanding that Jesus had in what He was to do in coming to this planet. Jesus mentions many things in His prayer, but there are four things I'd like to list from this great chapter:

1   I have finished the work (verse 4).

2. I have manifested Your name (verse 6).

3. I have given them Your word (verse 14).

4. I have declared Your name (verse 26).

JESUS REVIEWS HIS ASSIGNMENT
BEFORE THE FATHER

1. Jesus came to finish the work of the Father. Remember, it's the family business that Jesus continued in, touching and healing people's lives. *"If I do not do the works of My Father, do not believe Me"* (John 10:37). Encountering the work of the Father introduces that person to the Father Himself. *"Believe the works, that you may know and believe that the Father is in Me, and I in Him"* (John 10:38). That has been the nature and heart of God from day one. But it was never fully realized until Jesus.

2. *Jesus was a manifestation of the name of the Father.* Names reveal nature and identity. Jesus revealed the nature and identity of the Father. He lived in complete harmony with the name of the Father, confessing that He came in His name. (See John 5:43.) The miracles that Jesus performs are done in His Father's name. (See John 10:25.) The right and authority to become children of God was given to those who believe in His name, as He came in the name of His Father. (See John 1:12.)

3. *Jesus gave people the word of the Father.* Jesus was revealed as the Word of God. (See John 1:1.) He was described as the Word made flesh. (See John 1:14.) He only said what the Father was saying. He also said that those who hear His word and believe have eternal life. (See John 5:24.) Jesus then identifies the source of the word He spoke: *"If anyone loves Me, he will keep My word; and My Father will love him, and We will come to him and make Our home with him. He who does not love Me does not keep My words; and the word which you hear is not Mine but the Father's who sent Me"* (John 14:23–24). Remember that the worlds were created by the Word of God. Whenever He spoke, things were created. It's the same today. Saying what God is saying is one of the things we can do to release His life, love, and presence into the world around us.

4. *Jesus declared His name.* He already mentioned that He manifested His name. But now Jesus emphasizes that the name of the Father was also something that had to be declared. Some things must be proclaimed to have full effect. Jesus is the declaration from

Heaven as to who this Father is—He is exactly like Jesus! Page after page of the gospels we see Jesus declaring that all He said and did came from His Father. He took none of the glory for Himself, but, instead, made it known that He was merely declaring what had to be said.

It's a Clear Assignment

On several occasions, Beni and I have had foster children live with us for a season. On one of the more tragic occasions, we had two boys given to us whose parents had killed themselves. First it was the mom, because of abuse, and then, perhaps about six months later, the dad. Thankfully after a few weeks in our home their counselors said they didn't need counseling anymore. The children knew we loved them and they began to experience peace of heart and mind. But the first night or two in our home was quite interesting. When it came time to eat dinner, they grabbed all the food they could reach and wrapped their arms around their plates so that no one else could take it. They showed us how orphans live. We smiled and assured them they could have all they wanted, and that there would be more than enough again tomorrow. It took a little while, but soon they learned that provision was assured because they now lived with us.

Saying what God is saying is one of the things we can do to release His life, love, and presence into the world around us.

Orphans live differently from children who know they're loved. Self-preservation and self-promotion are not the driving points of the behavior of healthy children. Instead, the secure child is more inclined to celebrate the gift of another without fighting for the attention himself. All around us are orphans. It doesn't matter if we're talking about our neighbors, our bosses, our friends in church, or the conflict in the Middle East, or even the battle between political parties—we are being led and fed by orphans. They have no answers. They just have different ways of deadening the pain. People of God, now is the time to rise up. We have the privilege to know this wonderful Father for ourselves and deal once and for all with the part of us that wants, to hoard all the food on our plates. And from our personal victory we have the privilege to make Him known, giving the chance for others to experience Him for themselves.

Jesus gave the following assignment to His disciples: *"As the Father has sent Me, I also send you"* (John 20:21). Hopefully you can see by now that the assignment given to Jesus was to reveal the Father. In this passage, Jesus passes on this part of His assignment to us, and in doing so, He defines our purpose in much the same way as His. We still live in a world that He loves. This world is filled with people who will never really know their right hand from their left. The perspective on the values of Heaven only really comes to those who know the Father and that that Father is good.

Chapter Eight

JESUS CHRIST, PERFECT THEOLOGY

I still have questions for God...absolutely. But it is within faith, not outside faith, and surely not opposed to faith.
　　　　　　　　　　　　　　—ELI WIESEL

There is a deep, personal need in the Body of Christ to see Jesus for who He is. Jesus Christ is perfect in every way. He is perfect beauty, perfect majesty, perfect power, and perfect humility. The list of His wonderful characteristics and virtues is endless. But for the sake of this chapter, Jesus Christ is perfect theology—He is the will of God personified.

JESUS' RESPONSE TO PROBLEMS

Jesus healed all who came to Him, no exceptions. He also healed all the Father directed Him to heal. Setting another standard than what Jesus gave us is unacceptable.

Jesus stilled every life-threatening storm that He encountered. We never see Him using His authority to increase the impact of a storm or to bring calamity of any kind. Never once did He command the storm to destroy a city so that its citizens would become more humble and learn to pray, thus becoming more like Him. Today, many of our spiritual leaders announce why God sent the storm—to break the pride and sinfulness of a region. Obviously, God can use any tragedy to His purposes. But that doesn't mean the problem was His design. Jesus didn't deal with storms in that way. Regardless of how or why the storm came about, Jesus was the solution. In our world, many insurance companies and newspapers call natural disasters "acts of God." Perhaps, they got their theology from us.

Whatever you think you know about God that you can't find in the person of Jesus you have reason to question. Jesus Christ is the fullest and most precise revelation of the Father and His nature that could ever be made known.

By thinking that God causes our storms, diseases, and conflicts, are we resorting to the same reasoning as did James and John when they said, *"as Elijah did"*? (See Luke 9:54.) They justified their thinking by using an Old Testament standard for a New Testament dilemma. Are we truly justified for having such a response because we can find a biblical precedent in the Old Testament?

Why did Jesus rebuke the storm instead of just telling it to stop? The implication is that the powers of darkness were involved in the storm, and they needed to be dealt with because they violated the heart and purpose of God on the earth. And if the devil is involved in the storm, we don't want to be found saying the storm is the will of the Father.

Deliverance came to all who asked. This is Jesus. He illustrated this when the Syrophoenician woman came to Him on behalf of her daughter. (See Mark 7:24–30.) Jesus wasn't supposed to minister to her because she was a Gentile—His ministry was first to be offered to the Jew to fulfill the mandate of Scripture. This was a necessary step in order to open up the Gospel to every nation. Yet even here, we see that Jesus moved with the heart of compassion for people. He brought deliverance/healing to this young lady as a manifestation of the Father to a girl in need. Once again, Jesus revealed the Father exactly. And as a reminder, this is the work of the Holy Spirit upon Jesus, who lives in us to manifest the same.

Whatever you think you know about God that you can't find in the person of Jesus you have reason to question. Jesus Christ is the fullest and most precise revelation of the Father and His nature that could ever be made known.

There is a vast difference between the goodness of God seen in the life of Jesus and the goodness of God revealed through the belief system of the average church in the Western world. It has become easier for us to believe that either the standard Jesus set for our lives is metaphorical and therefore entirely unattainable for today or that it is theologically wrong to consider Jesus' example as a legitimate standard—it is historical only. At the root of the confusion is the difficulty in reconciling the differences in the life of Jesus and the experience of the everyday believer. To cover the discrepancies, we often create theology that keeps us comfortable, but also locked in perpetual immaturity. It has been easier to change our interpretation of Scripture by finding out why something didn't happen than it is to seek God *until* He answers with power.

JESUS' RESPONSE TO DISEASE

If Jesus healed everyone who came to Him, and the Father wills for people to be sick, then we have a divided house—one that, according to the teachings of Jesus, cannot stand. Invariably, it's at this point in the discussion that Old Testament verses are brought up in an attempt to prove that God causes the very things I suggest we are to bring answers to such things as sickness, storms, torment. And then we're told, "God changes not!" It's strange to me that this statement is used to prove that God continues to cause sickness but not to prove that, in the same way, Jesus healed everyone who came to Him. This is tragic because it is in His heart for us to do the same. It is true that God doesn't change. It's now important for us to see that He was the Merciful One in the Old as well as the New Testaments. It just wasn't until Jesus came that we got to see clearly what the Father was like.

> It's not that our belief systems change God. Our belief systems, or in this case *unbelief systems*, limit the activities of God in our lives.

We must ask ourselves how much of the Old Covenant we want to preserve. Is it a legitimate endeavor to preserve the standard of a God that causes our problems? Whatever we preserve is what we'll have to live under. It's not that our belief systems change God. Our belief systems, or in this case *unbelief systems*, limit the activities of God in our lives. There are severe warnings in Scripture about limiting God. *"How often they provoked Him in the wilderness, and grieved Him in the desert! Yes, again and again they tempted God, and limited the Holy One of Israel. They did not remember His power: the day when He redeemed them from the enemy"* (Ps. 78:40–42).

There are very few areas of the Christian life that the Church is willing to compromise on in this way, other than miracles, signs, and wonders. For example, we would never tell people to sacrifice sheep to atone for their sins. Jesus did that once, and for all. Neither would we make people travel to Jerusalem so they can be involved in acceptable worship to God. Jesus taught that present-day worship is not in a place, but is in Spirit and truth (see John 4:21–24). We would never think of forbidding those with physical deformities from coming before His presence in worship (see Lev. 21:18–21). Nor would we ever consider the blind as cursed by God (see Deut. 28:28). We will faithfully pray for the rebellious teenager, but we'd never stone that young person to death (see Deut. 21:18–21). Yet each of these statements represents God's dealings with people under the Old Covenant. Is it then not also true that these dealings with man reveal God's nature—one that changes not? God nearly killed Moses because he had not circumcised his sons. Yet for us, it is optional. We are now told to love our enemies, while in the Old Testament God commanded Israel to kill the enemy nations—every man, woman, and child. Elijah had eight hundred demon-possessed devil worshipers killed, yet Jesus gave Himself up for execution in the place of the wicked. Is it legal to continue to embrace those standards when Jesus came to reveal the Father more accurately? But historically, the Church has done this very thing with the subjects of healing and deliverance. If an Old Testament Scripture supersedes the perfect revelation of God found in Jesus Christ in the area of healing, then it also has that right in this list given above. Once again, we don't do this with any other part of the Gospel than we do with the realm of miracles, signs, and wonders. It is a present-day phenomenon—it has not always been this way.

It astounds me that the effort to be like Jesus can be so controversial. And strangely, the opposition comes from those who confess Christ. In this day, when people say we're to become Christ-like, they mean that we're to be patient, kind, and loving. The purity part of life is essential to being a faithful witness. But the power aspect is equal in importance. Purity and power are the two legs we stand on in giving witness to the resurrection of Jesus Christ, which is what we are witnesses of—the resurrection.

Two thousand years ago, all sickness was considered to be from the devil, and healing was from God—a sign of the present reality of God's Kingdom. Even something as simple as a fever was considered to be of the devil (see Mark 1:31). Things have disintegrated so far that many consider sickness to be sent or allowed by God to build our character, while those who pursue the ministry of healing are thought to be out of balance at best, and from the devil at worst. This is especially true if that person believes that everyone is to be healed. It's frightening to see how far things can fall in two thousand years. What is even more puzzling is that the very ones who consider the sickness to be approved or even sent by God for our benefit have no problem going to the doctor to find a cure and release from the disease. Such mindless approaches to Scripture must stop. And those who would never receive prayer for healing consider going to the doctor *common sense*. It may be *common*, but it lacks *sense* when it violates the example given to us in Scripture. Sometimes when we lack the experience mentioned in Scripture, we tend to look for an obscure passage that somehow explains and/or excuses our lack of experience in the place of the overwhelming evidence given through the life of Jesus.

For what it's worth, I have no problem with going to doctors or taking medicine. They can be used by God to bring about the intended result—health. You just can't have it both ways—believe that God sent a disease to teach us and then try to get rid of it through medical intervention. If that is your belief, you are violating the sovereignty of God. I do have a concern that so many live under the influence of "modern medicine" and give little or no thought to going to the Great Physician. I pray for healing but am willing to accept medical assistance, and I personally do that without shame.

Consider this: Many have been trained to embrace disease as a form of suffering for which we gain favor with God. If we can legitimately do that with sickness, we can do it with sin. Jesus paid the same price to render both realities powerless—see Psalm 103:3, Isaiah 33:24, Mark 2:9, and James 5:16.

JESUS CHRIST, THE MODEL FOR LIFE

As perfect theology, Jesus illustrates the will of God. He models how life is to be lived modeling the reality of His Kingdom. In this Kingdom, you live by dying, rise by going low, and receive by giving. The list of these logical contradictions seems endless. Yet they profoundly reveal His Kingdom—His heart. Below is a handful of areas that modeled how life is to be lived as it pertains to:

> **As perfect theology, Jesus illustrates the will of God. He models how life is to be lived modeling the reality of His Kingdom.**

Possessions—Jesus illustrates the heart of the Father in everything He says and does. He models our approach to possessions. I remind you He is God. He owns everything in Heaven and on earth. But His love is measured by what He gave—Himself. Jack Hayford defined abundance as being measured in what I've given away, not by what I have. Brilliant. Jesus modeled His value for excellence in wearing a seamless robe but kept a priority on caring for the poor and standing up for those who had no voice. Both Old and New Testaments illustrate that obedience can make a person prosperous. But Jesus brought a warning not often recognized in the Old—true riches, which are the unseen realities of the Kingdom for here and now, are better than money. And the love of money can cost us true riches.

Economics—Jesus illustrated the beauty of giving as the priority of the Kingdom finances. He also taught the power of contentment, knowing the lust for possessions is a cancer of the soul. But many make the mistake of thinking Jesus to be a socialist. Nothing could be further from the truth. He promises that for the disciples who left all to follow Him, they would receive one hundred times what they left—now, in this lifetime. (See Mark 10:28–30.) In His parables of the talents and minas (see Matt. 25:14–30; Luke 19:11–27), the person who would not responsibly work was left with nothing. And the part that is the most offensive in today's political climate is that Jesus took what little the irresponsible servant had and gave it to the person who had the most. Jesus Christ is not politically correct. But He is correct. Until I can see God's value for increase and heartily say "amen" to His decision in this story, I do not have His mind.

VIPs—Jesus models how to interact with important people. He never changed who He was or His message to appeal to famous people. He lived unmoved and unimpressed with position and title, yet served them like He would any other. He understands that all promotion comes from Him. Yet He made room for a religious leader named Nicodemus, who was afraid of the opinion of His peers, to come to Him in the night. This is a brilliant example of the Son of God standing firm in His laying down what it meant to follow Him, yet He had grace for those who had a heart to obey but lacked the courage needed in that moment. At the death of Christ it was Joseph of Arimathea who brought the spices for His burial and put the body of Jesus in his own tomb. The courageous death of Jesus imparted a courageous life for Joseph of Arimathea.

Satan—He didn't chase the devil. But He dealt with him when he got in the way of His redemptive purposes and lifestyle. He also never lived in reaction to the powers of darkness, but instead He lived in response to the Father. The devil loves the attention that many believers give him.

Religious Leaders—Jesus had little toleration for religious leaders who used their position for personal gain. Yet He welcomed honest conversation and interaction from those who were true to their call and displayed the necessary humility and hunger. He also acknowledged when they had great faith or wisdom in their conversations. (See Mark 12:34.)

Political Issues—He knew the hot political issues of His day and could have addressed any of them at any time. He taught on His Kingdom, which always aimed at the heart. Those teachings contained the answers needed to deal with the issues of His day and ours. He chose to provide instruction on how to thrive in less than ideal circumstances. For example, slavery: Jesus worked for all to become free. The Father was the one who created the concept of Jubilee, so that even in Old Testament times those who ended up in slavery due to poor decisions would always have the hope of becoming free. In the meantime, He helped slaves know how better to live in their tragic setting. Early in US history, people assumed His silence on this issue meant He supported slavery. Nothing could be further from the truth. He came to set people of every race free. Period. And while slavery is now illegal, many slaves still exist—to debt, bitterness, addictions—and in many parts of the world there is sex trafficking and, in some nations, actual slavery.

Sinners—Jesus showed us how to interact with people who were recognized by society as sinners. He spent time with them, but He didn't live the lifestyle of sin they were known for. He was called *the friend of sinners*. The religious leaders of the day criticized Jesus quite heavily because of the people He interacted with. It should be noted that sinners loved to be with Jesus but rarely like to be with us. And tragically, the believers that sinners often do like to be with do so because they practice the same compromising lifestyles that the unbeliever practices. Jesus was the holiest person ever to walk this planet. As such, He was still welcomed by sinners, which tells me that people have an ingrained appetite for true holiness. I'd like to suggest that love—real love—has that effect on people. It is what everyone is hungry for.

Angels—Jesus modeled the value of angels in His conversations and in His teaching. He was ministered to by angels in a place of fatigue and had them ascend and descend upon Him throughout His earthly life. But they were never worshiped or made the focal point of the life of a believer. I like to put it this way: angels are never to be worshiped—but neither are they to be ignored.

> **Jesus ruined every funeral He attended, including His own.**

Government—His approach to government is fascinating and right. We are to give Caesar what belongs to him in taxes, as governments serve a purpose in representing God in protecting and empowering people. I'm glad that Jesus walked the earth in a bad political season; otherwise, we would be able to say our allegiance to governments is only due when they are righteous.

Funerals—Jesus ruined every funeral He attended, including His own. His approach to death is noteworthy. Why did Jesus raise the dead? Because not everyone dies in God's timing. Therefore, it is important we take on His approach to this very serious subject and not so quickly assume that every death was in God's plan and purpose. The Bible says it is appointed for us to die (see Heb. 9:27). *"When?"* is the only question at hand, and we have a role in how that plays out.

THAT WHICH BRINGS US TOGETHER

All the prophets spoke of Jesus' coming. They served us well by announcing both His coming and the impact of His coming. The prophet Jeremiah gives us one of the most wonderful passages in this regard. Here is the impact:

> *"Therefore they shall come and sing in the height of Zion,*
> *Streaming to the goodness of the Lord*
> *For wheat and new wine and oil,*
> *For the young of the flock and the herd;*
> *Their souls shall be like a well-watered garden,*
> *And they shall sorrow no more at all.*
> *"Then shall the virgin rejoice in the dance,*
> *And the young men and the old, together;*
> *For I will turn their mourning to joy,*
> *Will comfort them,*
> *And make them rejoice rather than sorrow.*
> *"I will **satiate** the soul of the priests with **abundance**,*
> *And My people shall be satisfied with My goodness," says*
> *the Lord* (Jeremiah 31:12–14).

This passage excites me. The picture is so clear. The people of God will stream, flow like a river in one direction, to the goodness of the Lord. The Kingdom of God is the land of His goodness. This is the great discovery. His goodness is in itself an inexhaustible source of joy and delight. The word *satiate* means "to fill to the full." So here we see it: The priests—that is, every New Testament believer (see 1 Pet. 2:9)—are filled to the fullest, to a place of delight and complete satisfaction with the goodness of the Lord.

GOD'S GOODNESS IS ALWAYS EVIDENT

God sprinkled the entire Old Testament with evidence of His goodness, profoundly visible for those hungry enough to see it. He was setting the stage for the greatest revelation of all time—Jesus Christ. Jesus is a revelation of the heart and nature of God the Father. One of my favorite New Testament Scriptures on this theme speaks of how God revealed His heart throughout Old Testament times. It is one that deeply moves me, as it shows the heart of God reaching out to people before there is a relationship. It's found in Acts 14:17: *"Nevertheless He did not leave Himself without witness, in that He did good, gave us rain from heaven and fruitful seasons, filling our hearts with food and gladness."* Before we even come to know God as our Father, He is doing things to fill our hearts with gladness. That is amazing. It's His calling card. This simple approach by God is what He calls *leaving Himself a witness.* Consider this: A witness to an event of any kind is someone who speaks not from hearsay, but from personal experience, from firsthand knowledge of the subject at hand. When God leaves Himself a witness, He is drawing each person to Himself to experience His favor. His desire is for that favor to awaken a longing in their hearts to know Him as their Father. He will not force Himself upon us, as He continues to work to protect one of the most glorious parts of His creation—the free will of mankind. Yet, in His longing for us, He draws us to Himself through the blessings that can only come from a good Father.

In representing the Father in the Sermon on the Mount, Jesus made a startling statement, following it with an even more startling question: *"If you then, being evil, know how to give good gifts to your children, how much more will your Father who is in heaven give good things to those who ask Him!"* (Matt. 7:11). Jesus acknowledges that it is possible for evil people to do good things. But He uses that as the backdrop for an amazing revelation of the nature and heart of the Father. All of us have sinned. And even in a sinful state we are capable of doing good things for our children. On the other hand, God is the ultimate in perfect holiness and purity. He has never sinned in action, not even in thought or intent. Jesus challenges us to use our imagination to consider the goodness of His Father as compared to ours by asking, *"How much more will your Father who is in heaven give good things to those who ask Him!"* That moves me deeply. The question, "How much more?" is the one left echoing in my heart. And it has to do with a Father not merely meeting basic needs. That is a given. He knows what we need before we ask and has promised to care for us. (See Matthew 6:8.) This time He is speaking of a Father who meets the cries and, more importantly, the dreams of the hearts of His children. The word used for *good things* is fascinating. It means *that which produces benefits* and implies *attractiveness and excellence.* As you can see, this is far beyond meeting basic needs. He is a loving Father, not the caretaker of an orphanage, guaranteeing us three meals a day and a cot to sleep on at night. His approach to us is based entirely on who He is—perfect in holiness, beauty, wisdom, understanding, and love. He has big-time love for all His children that is demonstrated by His giving gifts to them according to who they are and what's in their hearts. Remember, this is preceded by a question that is eternal and without limits—*How much more?*

BLESS WHAT HE BLESSES

One of the things that is sometimes hard to get used to is that God loves to bless both the righteous and the unrighteous. We celebrate the times when God gives a brilliant insight to a believer. Whether that insight cures a disease, or makes possible a new invention that will serve mankind well, or brings peace between two nations in conflict through His beloved peacemaker, it's something that we are all encouraged to hear about. I believe He is affirming the gifts and callings of this servant of the Lord and is using him or her in a profound way to increase the witness of His heart for people. But it must also be acknowledged that He sometimes chooses to do the same through unbelievers who at times are extremely wicked in lifestyle and even purpose. What is God doing by giving such treasure to the wicked? Leaving a witness.

One of the more frightening examples of this in Scripture is with Herod. He gave a speech to a crowd that was not inclined to idolize him yet kept shouting, *"'The voice of a god and not of a man!' Then immediately an angel of the Lord struck him, because he did not give glory to God. And he was eaten by worms and died"* (Acts 12:22–23). Consider this: He was killed because he did not give glory to God for his ability to impact the crowd profoundly with his speech. That implies that it was the grace of God that was upon him to speak something meaningful to the people. God anointed him. This is especially hard for the Church to recognize in this hour. Political tensions are high, and if someone doesn't boldly confess a born-again experience in Christ, and then model it in a Mother Theresa-type fashion, the Church is likely to criticize and reject that individual. It's become hard for us to recognize the anointing that rests upon people who sometimes are not believers. This is especially true if that person doesn't meet our personal criteria for a leader. If the person has made moral and political blunders in his past, there's little chance the Church will see the hand of God upon him for His appointed time. Seeing through the eyes of a perfect Father, who always has redemptive purposes in all He does, is necessary in this hour.

The bottom line is, that the anointing of God can rest upon ungodly people for divine purposes. We see that again with Caiaphas, the high priest, in John 11:49–52. He prophesied about the crucifixion of Christ and the effects it would have on the nation of Israel. He declared the Word of the Lord, not from his relationship with God, but because of his position. There are times when God rests upon a life entirely for the person—the calling card of blessing. And sometimes that grace is upon the person for the sake of the people he serves or influences, as was the case with Caiaphas. It's our job to recognize it if we intend to see the full effect of His *calling card* upon society.

Jesus taught us in the Sermon on the Mount, *"But I say to you, love your enemies, bless those who curse you, do good to those who hate you, and pray for those who spitefully use you and persecute you, that you may be sons of your Father in heaven; for He makes His sun rise on the evil and on the good, and sends rain on the just and on the unjust"* (Matt. 5:44–45). God's approach is to show favor and blessing to all. If we want to emulate this wonderful Father, proving that we are truly sons of our Father, we must love those who have not earned it. This is the heart of God. It proves to be a vital part of understanding how this Kingdom works. If He chooses to give favor to the most wicked among us, who am I to choose to condemn and reject? I must bless what He blesses, knowing He is leaving His mark upon the hearts of people in a way that He chooses, the way that He knows works best.

When He reveals our absolute lost condition because of sin, He does so that we might turn from sin and receive His solution— forgiveness unto adoption.

I love to hear stories of people who have had unusual favor or blessing come into their lives that changed everything for the rest of their lives. Oftentimes, these types of experiences will make the headlines. Tears often come to my eyes when I hear of how God has left a mark of favor on a person's life long before he could earn it. These stories almost always include the unusual coincidence or what some might call a twist of fate. In reality, they are God leaving His calling card, the one that shouts His goodness, so that He might be known as the Father of all that is right in the world. In this way, He summons people into an eternal destiny of delight, if they care enough to slow down, recognize the source, saying "yes" to the only One with the right to rule their lives; and rule He does—right into the greatest freedoms imaginable.

God is God, and He will always do as He pleases. He is not subject to us and never owes us an explanation for anything, although He freely gives Himself to us over and over again. It's not as though my description of His goodness puts us in a position of control or judgment. On the contrary, all that I have written to this point is simply to declare that the cornerstone of all theology is the goodness of God. For me that means that no matter what happens, the one thing I don't question is His goodness. I may never understand how or why something happens. I will not sacrifice my knowledge of the goodness of God on the altar of human reasoning so that I can have an explanation for why a tragedy has happened. But one thing is for sure: He is good—and He is always better than I think.

Chapter Nine

It's Not His Fault

Why, then, did God give them free will? Because free will, though it makes evil possible, is also the only thing that makes possible any love or goodness or joy worth having.

—C.S. LEWIS, *Mere Christianity*

God is usually blamed for the evils that exist in the world because if He is God, He can remove any problem quite easily because He is big and powerful. But to rid the world of sin and its consequences would require something extremely dramatic—removing all sinners. And apart from being born again, how many of us would be left? C.S. Lewis once made a statement that has helped me quite a bit throughout the years—*"once the author steps on the stage, the play is over."* He can fix it all in a moment. But when He does, time stops, eternity begins, and the final line has been drawn in the sand. His answer would be quite painful. His patience, which we see in full operation right now, is so that we can gather as many into the family as possible. His longsuffering is beyond all of our abilities to comprehend and comes at great personal cost. Fixing this world's problems through a "military invasion of Heaven" is not the answer we want. For then He enforces His will over mankind, destroying the greatest of all creations called the free will. In doing so, He would then forfeit the chance to have a people of divine purpose. He chose instead an invasion of love, where the hearts of people are conquered by One who sacrifices fully for their well-being. As a result, we now have a Gospel of power that solves the issues at hand quite well, enabling us to bring that same message to them that changed us forever. We now just need people who believe it, live it, and will risk all to display it.

Jesus displayed the heart of His Father perfectly in every possible situation. It didn't matter whether it was disease, tormenting demons, storms, mothers with dead children, crowds with nothing to eat, or one of the numerous other calamities recorded in the Gospels. Each situation became an opportunity to reveal what the God of the universe was really like. Time and time again, we are left awestruck when He is manifested as the Father we would all dream of having if we had the ability to dream in that measure. Was this display of miracles a temporary exhibition of His kindness? Many think so. For them, it was God becoming manifest in that way until the canon of Scripture was completed. If that weren't so sad, that idea would be laughable.

I'm so thankful for the Scriptures, the absolute Word of God. The Word of God is given for our instruction. In receiving it, we become equipped, empowered, and directed to a lifestyle that displays and fulfills the will of God on earth. It is this same Word of God that reveals Jesus as the will of God. In fact, Jesus is the Word of God made flesh (see John 1:14), the perfect revelation of the will of God. How can it be acceptable to be devoted to the Word of God (the Bible) and not the Word of God (the person)? Jesus healed on the Sabbath because to the Father people were more important than how the religious leaders interpreted the rules. Some seem to think He has gone back to prioritizing religious leaders' interpretations of the rules, where misguided instruction speaks louder than the voice of compassion reaching out to the people in need. People are still His treasure, found in the field He purchased. The Kingdom Now was and is His answer. Love requires the display of His answers now.

Jesus was the fulfillment of an ongoing revelation of the heart of the Father. This revelation only increases from season to season. It's the principle given to us from Isaiah 9:7: *"There will be no end to the increase of His government or of peace."* It only increases—goes forward. The concept of ongoing forward motion is repeated in 2 Corinthians 3:18: *"from glory to glory."* The point is, God takes us forward in an ever-increasing revelation. It never declines or goes back to inferior standards, especially those of the Old Testament. Once the demands of the Old were met (in and by Jesus), the New came into prominence permanently. Once the real has become manifest (i.e., Jesus, the Lamb of God), we never go back to the symbolic (sacrificing sheep). Once the Kingdom has become manifest, there's no going back. If Jesus opened up the revelation of the Father through miracles, signs, and wonders, why would He then return to the inferior? He didn't. We did. And that's the point. To make sure we'd never forget the standard He set, He stated the impossible: *"Most assuredly, I say to you, he who believes in Me, the works that I do he will do also; and greater works than these he will do, because I go to My Father"* (John 14:12). Forward motion—that's the plan of God. No retreat. And, no excuses.

WHAT'S IN YOUR WALLET?

I can die of starvation with a million dollars in the bank. If I don't make withdrawals from what's in my account, my wealth is no better than a dream, principle, or fantasy. Everything in our account in Christ is beyond our wildest dreams. We can't make a withdrawal if we don't know what exists. Jesus models the mere beginning of what's in our account. The promises of His Word give us even greater insight into this superior reality. It's time to see what Jesus has so we can see what Jesus gave us. Here's the bottom line—He gave us everything that belongs to Him. And the Father gave Him everything! Look at it here in John 16:14–15, speaking of the work of the Holy Spirit—"*He will glorify Me, for He will take of what is Mine and declare it to you. All things that the Father has are Mine. Therefore I said that He will take of Mine and declare it to you.*"

Everything in our account in Christ is beyond our wildest dreams. We can't make a withdrawal if we don't know what exists.

This really is an amazing passage of Scripture, one for which we bear great responsibility. The Holy Spirit releases what Jesus alone possesses into our accounts through declaration. Every time He speaks to us, He transfers the eternal resources of Jesus to our account, enabling us to complete our assignment: *"Heal the sick, cleanse the lepers, raise the dead, cast out demons. Freely you have received, freely give. …Go therefore and make disciples of all the nations, baptizing them in the name of the Father and of the Son and of the Holy Spirit, teaching them to observe all things that I have commanded you; and lo, I am with you always, even to the end of the age"* (Matt. 10:8; 28:19–20). Notice it says for the disciples to teach their converts all that Jesus taught them. That *must* include the instruction to heal the sick, cast out devils, etc. There was never to be a discrepancy between how we live today and His initial standard.

When Jesus worked in miracles, was He merely creating an appetite in us to be in Heaven for eternity? Heaven should always remain something we are passionate about. It was Jesus who taught us how to pray, *"On earth as it is in heaven"* (see Matt. 6:10). Yes, eternity is important. But going to Heaven is not my responsibility. He will get me there, entirely by His grace. My job is very specific and extremely important—bring Heaven to earth through prayer and obedience. Please notice that when Jesus declared the Kingdom was at hand, He displayed it by giving life, breaking the powers of darkness, and restoring broken lives, hearts, and homes. He told us to pick up the same message. Why should we expect a different outcome?

Many years ago, I read a wonderful book entitled *Kingdom Now, But Not Yet*, written by Tommy Reid, an amazing pastor and apostolic leader from Buffalo, New York. He was one of the main speakers at a conference in Portland, Oregon, I attended in the eighties. I was powerfully impacted by his teaching and then by his book. Both the title and content spoke to me deeply. I had never heard the phrase before that he used as the title of his book. It had a great impact on me because, while we live with the obvious reality of the "not yet," he introduced me to more of the "now" part of the Kingdom I had not been aware of in the measure God intended.

I realize that this is probably a personal frustration, but most of the time I cringe when I hear that phrase being used today. The reason is that I almost always hear it used to describe what we can't have now, instead of announcing what God has made available for us in this great day we live in. It's become an excuse instead of an invitation. That being said, we do live in both realities—the Kingdom is now and is to come more fully in the future. But realizing that there were generations before us that had greater breakthroughs than we've seen in our lifetime should help us recognize that there is more. Much more, designed for right now. I remind you, the increase of His government (manifestation of His rule/Kingdom) never ends! Today should always be greater than yesterday.

THE WILL OF GOD

The great Bible teacher Bob Mumford wrote a wonderful book entitled *The King and You.*[1] It was here I learned something about the will of God that has helped me immensely. There are two different words used in the original language of the New Testament for the word *will*, referring in this case to the *will of God*. One is the word, *boulema,* and the other is *thelema*. Boulema refers to that which is established and fixed in the will of God. That is the *will of God* which will happen regardless of who believes it, or who opposes it. The return of Christ falls into that Category. One example is in 2 Peter 3:9, *"God is not willing that any should perish."* And yet people are perishing. Paul could have used *thelema* referring to God's desire or wish for people to repent. Instead he uses *boulema* to make sure we understand that *God has not willed* for people to perish. The word *thelema* is quite different in that it refers to God's desires and wishes. For example, *"and do not be conformed to this world, but be transformed, by the renewing of your mind, so that you may prove what the will of God is, that which is good acceptable and perfect"* (Romans 12:2 NASB). Here the renewed mind is able to fulfill and reveal the desires of God. When we think and see from God's perspective, we become enabled to see His heart, and manifest His intentions.

This is huge. God has desires that may or may not be fulfilled. Make no mistake. He has the power to make anything happen that He wants to happen. But He has the heart to work with the process of the development of His people to take responsibility and co-labor with Him. The outcome of this process is we become a people who look and live like His Son, Jesus.

The first word for the will of God, *boulema*, that I mentioned previously is referring to things that are unchangeable. For example, Jesus is coming back. You can vote *yes, no,* or *I don't care.* It matters not. We don't have a role in that decision. It is put entirely in the hands of the Father, who alone determines how and when that event will happen. On the other hand, there are many things that God would like to have happen, and has made possible, but they never will be, because believers either don't believe they are the will of God anymore or they are waiting for God Himself to do them. That will is represented with the word *thelema.* I remind you of the time Jesus told the disciples to feed the multitude of thousands when they had nothing but a child's lunch. Jesus never took back His commission to do it Himself when they said they were unable to accomplish that impossible task. He still set the stage for them to see the miracle through their hands as they handed out the food. And they did. (See Mark 6:37–44.)

> **The will of God has been a much-debated subject, which I often find quite entertaining. It does us no good to keep the conversation in a classroom caught up in Christian theory. It has to be taken onto the streets, where the hurting people are.**

The will of God has been a much-debated subject, which I often find quite entertaining. It does us no good to keep the conversation in a classroom caught up in Christian theory. It has to be taken onto the streets, where the hurting people are. The will of God must be displayed by a praying people, unwilling to sit on the sidelines and see the devil continually steal, kill, and destroy, and then watch the theorist give God the credit. Masking our unbelief with a spineless theology is the great deception. This continual misrepresentation of the nature and heart of God for one another and for the world must stop. Stupidity often looks like intelligence in the absence of experience.

WHO IS IN CONTROL?

One of the most common phrases used in this discussion is that "God is in control." It is true that He is the Sovereign God. He reigns over all, and everything belongs to Him. Nothing is outside of His reach or His concern. He is all-knowing and all-powerful. But is He in control? This is not a question of His ability or His power and authority. If He is, doesn't that make Him responsible for Hitler? Is brain cancer His idea? If He is in control, then we have to credit Him with disease, earthquakes, hurricanes, and all the other calamities in life. You get the point. I think it's more accurate to say He is in charge, but He is not in control. Every parent reading this should get this point quite easily. While we are in charge of our homes, not everything that happens under our roof is necessarily our idea or is approved by us. This is an important distinction.

VAIN BABBLING

It has never seemed right to me to hear Christians talk about a tragedy and then say, "It must have been the will of God, or it wouldn't have happened." Or more specifically, "Isn't it tragic for such a young man to die in that car wreck, leaving his wife and small children? But we know God works in mysterious ways." Or worse yet, "We don't know why it was God's will for that child to die, but we know God has a reason." These conversations are actually quite common—they've become normal in many settings. As heartbreaking as the disaster is, the response of believers is equally appalling, in my thinking. There's the assumption that if God wanted a different outcome, He would have made it happen. That is lazy theology that somehow releases us from responsibility by shifting the blame to a God who put us in charge. I realize that the "us in charge" is where many will have conflict with me on this subject. I'm not sure how far to take this. Reason this through for yourself, but at least consider this: Jesus gave us a model to follow. He illustrated the will of God when facing problems. He also gave us His authority to accomplish our great assignment/commission successfully, which included teaching all future followers of Jesus the things that were taught and modeled by Jesus Himself. He followed that with the instruction to make sure all followers would be clothed with power—the Holy Spirit. The Holy Spirit is the resurrection power of Jesus. He made the same power available for every believer that was in the life of Jesus Christ, the Son of God, the Son of Man. Then Jesus returned to the Father, saying that we would see greater works than He did. (See John 14:12.) Do I take the assumption too far? Perhaps. But neither Jesus nor His disciples ever modeled the above reasoning of accepting a problem as the will of God. So whom did Jesus leave behind with the same tools of authority, power, and presence to deal with the threats of crisis, tragedy, disease, and disasters that He had? Us. We may not have all the responsibility when there are threats of horrific problems headed our way, but we do have some. And it's time to find out how to use the tools we've been given, and more specifically, to find out how to cooperate with the Holy Spirit in a way that brings glory to the name of Jesus in the earth, instead of making theological excuses.

As I've already stated, God can work any situation around for His glory. He is that good. And I'm thankful. I've witnessed the most horrific things happen to people, and I've seen them turn to this Father of grace and have watched as God has healed their hearts to a place of unexplainable strength. But to credit Him as the cause of the problem because He can use it redemptively is illogical and foolish. It violates the nature of God revealed in Jesus Christ. The fruit of such confusion within the family about the nature of our Father is a world around us that is even more confused about the nature of this God we have claimed wants to save them.

God has desires, wishes, and dreams. He brought us into a relationship with Him as a part of that dream. None of us were forced into this relationship with God. Now we have a position in Christ to help bring about more of His desire by having influence on what happens and what doesn't happen on planet Earth. For example, consider this very simple illustration. We carry the message of salvation. This message must be preached in all the world. If we send preachers of this message to one nation, but refuse to send any to another, there will be many times the amount of converts in the nation we chose to serve with the Gospel. Does it mean that God willed the others to miss out on eternal life? No. We did. That was our choice. God is *"not willing that any should perish but that all should come to repentance"* (2 Pet. 3:9b). What is God's will in this passage? That no one would perish in their sins, but that *all* would come to repentance. That is the will of God. Is it happening? No. Is it His fault? No. Does that mean that He is lacking the ability to bring about His desire? No. He made it possible for all to come to Christ. He gave us an example to follow in Jesus. He made us sinless through the blood of Jesus. He then commissioned us by Jesus. Then He empowered us with the same power that Jesus had in His earthly ministry. He made it possible for the will of God to be done on earth as it is in Heaven. The catalyst of that becoming reality is a people who pray—relentlessly pray—what He told us to pray: *"on earth as it is in heaven"* (see Matt. 6:10).

Let me give an example of this mystery. One of the great stories in John took place at the pool of Bethesda. I've been to the remains of that pool in Israel. And while it's not one that gathers great crowds, it is in some ways my favorite site in all of Israel. God seems to stir my heart there more than almost every other site. Here is the story:

> *Now there is in Jerusalem by the Sheep Gate a pool, which is called in Hebrew, Bethesda, having five porches. In these lay a great multitude of sick people, blind, lame, paralyzed, waiting for the moving of the water. For an angel went down at a certain time into the pool and stirred up the water; then whoever stepped in first, after the stirring of the water, was made well of whatever disease he had. Now a certain man was there who had an infirmity thirty-eight years. When Jesus saw him lying there, and knew that he already had been in that condition a long time, He said to him, "Do you want to be made well?" The sick man answered Him, "Sir, I have no man to put me into the pool when the water is stirred up; but while I am coming, another steps down before me." Jesus said to him, "Rise, take up your bed and walk." And immediately the man was made well, took up his bed, and walked* (John 5:2–9).

This is such a beautiful story of a man without hope being touched by the compassion of Jesus. Jesus came to him representing the heavenly Father. It's priceless. If this story were to happen today, there would be initial excitement by some. But the newspaper columnists, the TV anchors, the theologians, pastors, and teachers would be interviewing the people that were around the pool that weren't healed. I'm told there easily could have been up to one thousand people or more gathered around that pool, hoping for their chance at a miracle by getting into the pool after the angel stirred the water. The interview would go something like this: "How did it feel to have Jesus walk past you to heal someone else?" Some would use that platform to warn people of the danger of getting their hopes up, as the camera sweeps across the crowd of lame and diseased people. Many of those who represent the Church would then come to the conclusion that while this one act may have been from God, it is rather obvious evidence that it is not God's will to heal everyone. Why? Instead of trying to show us what God could do, He was trying to show us what one man could do who had no sin and was completely empowered by the Holy Spirit. If we're that concerned about this pool surrounded by sick people, *Go! "Go into all the world..."* (Mark 16:15).

This will of God is not complicated. Jesus is the will of God. He points to a perfect Father. And that Father has great dreams and desires for each of us. We are in His heart of dreams. And those dreams are for both now and eternity. Taking the time to consider Him and think according to His heart and His nature will have a dramatic effect on what we see and experience during our lifetime. We owe it to everyone around us to consider Him as He is—a good and perfect Father.

NOTE

1.   Bob Mumford, *The King and You* (1974, Revell Publishing, Ada, MI).

Chapter Ten

RE-PRESENTING THE GOODNESS OF GOD

The greatest issue facing the world today, with all its heartbreaking needs, is whether those who, by profession or culture, are identified as "Christians" will become disciples—students, apprentices, practitioners—of Jesus Christ, steadily learning from Him how to live the life of the Kingdom of the Heavens into every corner of human existence.

—DALLAS WILLARD

When Jesus taught His disciples to pray, He gave them a list of principles to guide them. They are found in what is commonly called the Lord's Prayer. That's not really a good title for the prayer because in the prayer is the confession of sin, and Jesus had no sin. It could more accurately be called the Disciple's Prayer. As such, it is a profound example of the kinds of things we're to put both our attention and affection on in prayer. Perhaps the most important lesson learned is that the Kingdom of God becomes manifest through prayer.

The things listed are *the most important things* from God's point of view. If you're interested in a study of this prayer, I wrote more thoroughly on it in my book *When Heaven Invades Earth*. But there's one thing I want to pull out for examination here, as it helps us in this journey of discovering God as a perfect Father. The prayer begins with, *"Our Father."* And it ends with *"For Yours is the kingdom...Amen."* Look at the point being made. It's a Father's kingdom. In other words, all conversation about kingdom is about family. And once we've left the subject of family, we've left the subject of kingdom. This, of course, is bigger than our biological families. It is about a Father who lovingly serves the purpose and benefit of all that He has made, all for His glory.

GOD IS REALLY GOOD

Believing that God is good is absolutely vital to becoming effective in the ministry of the Gospel. Our endurance in representing Jesus well and consistently is dependent on this one thing. God is absolute goodness.

The apostle Paul taught us to prophesy according to our faith (see Rom. 12:6). This is amazing—faith has an effect on *what* we prophesy. This explains many of the words of judgment that continually flow from some of our leaders. It is easier to prophesy judgment than reformation when our confidence is in the power of sin and its effects instead of the power of the Gospel. Society naturally declines in the absence of a great outpouring of the Spirit. And if our prophets, who both "foretell" and "cause," forsake the responsibility to declare the purposes of God with their words, then what are we to expect? In part, the prophetic ministry "causes" change by declaring such change. That is why the Scriptures state, *"Death and life are in the power of the tongue"* (Prov. 18:21). That does not give us license to fantasize about what we'd like to see happen in our lifetime. But it does give us the responsibility to search the Scriptures to find the heart of God and declare accordingly.

Some things actually come about because of the faith of those who have gained a place of authority to declare. Both Abraham and Moses illustrate this truth beautifully. They shaped the course of history through their friendships with God. Those who simply identify the errors of the day do little more for us than do our newspapers and TV newscasts.

When the disciples wanted to call down fire on the Samaritans "like Elijah did," Jesus told them they didn't know what spirit they were of (see Luke 9:51–55). To me, He's saying, "You can't do that with My anointing. You'll have to get that from another spirit, because to bring destruction in My name because people reject Me isn't Me. It is demonic in origin." And yet, the great prophet Elijah, anointed by God, did the very thing they wanted to do. He was the example for such an act. Jesus really meant it when He said He came to fulfill the prophets (see Matt. 5:17). He bore the judgment upon His own flesh that should have been released over all the cities of the earth. He made this hour possible where we have the privilege to release life, hope, and a future.

I am not impressed with those who tell me they watched the buildings burn on 9/11 and knew in their hearts that such calamity would not bring revival to America. Is that prophetic insight? Or have we become so impressed with darkness that we contribute to the problem with our declarations, prayers, and negative responses? Is He not the "desire of the nations"? If so, what is the missing element?

Could it be we need to be a Church that believes it's possible to accomplish the very assignment Jesus gave us in the nations? (See Matthew 28:19.) Shouldn't we then become a people that believes the entire harvest field is harvestable now? Is that not what Jesus was addressing when He declared *"the fields…are white to harvest"* (John 4:35)?

THE NEED FOR BURNING CONVICTION

Without a conviction of God's goodness, it's not possible to develop the clear focus and the strength of faith to pursue the breakthroughs that the earth itself aches for. How we see Him defines how we think and how we live. The way we understand Him *is* the way we will re-present Him. When I talk about the goodness of God and His greatness displayed in Jesus, I don't forget that He was also the one who chased the moneychangers out of the temple with a whip. This, too, is love, as Jesus hates whatever misrepresents the Father! The religious leaders of His day used their position for personal gain instead of in service of the people.

> **How we see Him defines how we think and how we live. The way we understand Him *is* the way we will re-present Him.**

In the same way, it is a misrepresentation of the Father to say He permits sickness to discipline us. This is not true anymore than it is to say He uses sin to discipline His children. For sickness is to my body what sin is to my soul. It's time for those moneychangers to get chased out of the temple.

When we understand the nature of this truth, we see that Jesus is not warring against the Father to reveal Himself as a new and improved standard of God. He is accurately revealing and manifesting the nature of the Father, as He has always been.

We can either create a doctrine that allows for lack or seek God until Heaven comes according to promise. The only time we know of that the disciples didn't get a miracle breakthrough was in their attempt to bring deliverance and healing to a child that was being thrown into the fire for his destruction. (See Mark 9:14–29.) They had no reason to think that they couldn't bring about the deliverance that the father requested, as it had always worked in the past. The absence of an answer was so surprising to them that they asked Jesus why they couldn't bring about the breakthrough for this family. In other words, they expected it. An environment of expectation naturally creates a question that has to be answered. We owe it to ourselves and the people we love to find out "why" when a breakthrough doesn't come. He gave them insight into the effects of prayer and fasting on such deeply rooted demonic situations. While the answer Jesus gave offers us great insight, the part that often gets overlooked is that *when you don't get an answer, get alone with Jesus, and find out why.* Not getting answers is not acceptable, nor is it to become normal. The life of the believer is not to be measured by unanswered prayers. It's quite the opposite. The fruit grown on the vine in John 15 is at least in part an answer to prayer. (See John 15:7–8.) For many, it's just become easier to blame God by calling it the "mysterious will of God" than it is to accept the fact that we've not arrived yet and get alone with God. Let's face it, we are all in process, yet we remain the ones He left in charge.

The story of this demonized child is one that hits me deeply. I'll never forget a young mother who brought her little boy to me that was being tormented by a demon. This happened close to twenty years ago while I was ministering in Southern California. The torment was very real and very dark. The demon manifested through the child as I prayed. I did all I knew to do. Dealing with demons was not new to me, as I had been involved in a ministry that had to deal with this fairly often. I responded to the need with compassion and all the authority I had—to no avail. I'll never forget the look on her face when her child wasn't helped. It had to be similar to the father of the child that the disciples couldn't help. Her disappointment screamed, "Is this all there is? Is this all you have?" She then asked me, "What do I do now?" I gave her the best counsel I could. But it felt pretty shallow to me, as I'm sure it did to her. The outcome of this child going home without help is unacceptable, and can in *no way* be called the will of God. It just didn't turn out the way it was supposed to. Prayer and fasting was in order. I wonder how often people leave our churches after receiving prayer without a breakthrough and assume their problem is somehow the mysterious will of God. Or worse yet, the one who is doing the ministry assumes the problem is in God's plan for their lives and then creates a theology around what didn't happen.

IT'S ALL ABOUT JESUS

Few people have issues with Jesus. They may not like the church, religion, or those who confess a born-again experience, but few actually reject Jesus. They may not accept that He is the Son of God, but most at least admire what Jesus stood for. I have my doubts that Jesus is offended with this common lack of insight into His identity, as His disciples were unclear on this issue early in their journey. As someone once put it, "The disciples belonged before they believed." Those who spent time with Him were always changed by the ongoing encounter and relationship. Those who fail to see who He is clearly just need an encounter with people who authentically represent Him. Encounters with Him are filled with purity, power, glory, and most of all love that is sacrificial in nature.

Jesus is the model provided for us. He is the eternal Son of God. But the part that is difficult to understand and impossible to explain is that He is totally God and totally man. It's the great mystery. The part that is vital to see and understand is that Jesus did nothing as God. He chose to live with the restrictions of a man. For this reason He said, *"The Son can do nothing of Himself"* (John 5:19). The cutting edge of this revelation is that Jesus gave us an example. Even though He is the eternal Son of God, He chose to live with the limitations of a man so that He might give us something to follow. Let's face it, if Jesus did all His miracles as God, I'm still impressed. But that is an impossible example for me to follow. I am simply an observer, which I'm very happy with, *if* that's His purpose for my life. I have no problem celebrating the amazing things that only God can do. But from the beginning, it has been God who continually sets the stage to partner with imperfect people in a co-laboring relationship. When I see that He did what He did as a man following His Father, then I am compelled to do whatever I need to do to follow that example. I am no longer content to live as I am. I will still celebrate His goodness, but now it will be from the very "trenches" that Jesus lived in.

There are two conditions put upon me in Jesus' example. These qualifications are essential for me to emulate the life, presence, and power that Jesus made evident. First is the fact that Jesus had no sin. Without Jesus, I was hopelessly lost in sin. But I am no longer without Him, and never will be again. That lost condition is no longer a factor, nor is it my identity. Now I am found in Christ, without sin, because His blood has made me clean. Because of such overwhelming mercy and grace, I have met the first qualification. The second condition is that Jesus was entirely empowered by the Holy Spirit. As a man, He was powerless. But the Spirit of God came upon Him in His water baptism. (See Luke 3:21–22.) It was right after that experience that we see Him walking in power. (See Luke 4:1,14.) When Jesus wanted His disciples to live in the same power that He did, He had them wait in Jerusalem so that they might receive what was promised—the same outpouring of the Holy Spirit He received, now to be released upon them all. (See Acts 1:8; 2:1–4.)

Jesus' life was an illustration of what one man could do who had no sin and was entirely empowered by the Holy Spirit. Jesus, who was entirely God, modeled life with the limitations of a man.

The reality of Jesus' success in ministry doesn't change because not everyone I pray for gets healed. He is the standard, not me. He is the leader, and I'm learning to follow. Any discrepancies are on my end, not His.

It's a theological crime to change the intent and message of the Scriptures in order to make me feel comfortable with my ministry experience. Lowering the standard of the Bible to the level of my experience should nauseate all of us. It is wrong. Some compensate by taking responsibility for the miraculous that is beyond the mandate of Scripture, resulting in shame and guilt. Both shame and guilt are self-focused. The ministry of miracles is Christ-focused. Shame and guilt are efforts of the enemy to get us to take unnatural responsibility for what God has called us to do—heal the sick, etc., as though it were in our ability to do so (see Matt. 10:8). He tries to lead us into even greater frustration for the impossible call of God upon our lives, as frustration ends in unbelief. You don't have to look very far away to see that conclusion. Those responses do nothing to take us deeper in the ministry of breakthrough. Taking biblical responsibility for what He has called us to do is good and right, *if* it takes us to Him. Nothing else will do.

If I were to define my life in extremely simple terms, it would be this—I cry out to God for increasing breakthroughs in private, and then I learn to take risks in public. If there is breakthrough, I give

God all the glory. If there isn't a breakthrough, I go back to that private place in prayer and cry out to God once again. That of course is followed once again with risk in public. That is the cycle for my life.

A WORD BORN IN COURAGE

Courage is one of the manifestations of the *dunamis* power that was made available to the Church on the Day of Pentecost. Courage enables the people of God to speak with a boldness that brings God into the moment. This is how we give Him something to "amen" to: We declare what He is saying with boldness, and He shows up to demonstrate His will in response to the claims of our message.

> It's a theological crime to change the intent and message of the Scriptures in order to make me feel comfortable with my ministry experience.

Demonstrating His will requires risk. *"And they went out and preached everywhere, the Lord working with them, confirming the word through the accompanying signs"* (Mark 16:20). Much of what is presently taught and confessed by the Church can be accomplished apart from God. It appeals to human talent and skill and can be accomplished through personal discipline and common goals. While these things are still important, they are secondary to what we've been called to address in the realm of impossibility. If Jesus had preached what is preached in most North American pulpits on any given Sunday, He never would have been crucified. Correct words attract Heaven and infuriate the powers of darkness. While the powers of darkness are not to be the focus of our message, their influence must be confronted and threatened by our declarations.

Rallying together with human talent to accomplish any given project for the Lord satisfies that inner need for community, focus, and discipline. It is good. But it will never satisfy our longing to see the impossibilities of life bend their knee to the name of Jesus. The Lord is provoking us to a courage that is anchored on His eternal purpose for His Bride. In Acts 4:29–30, Peter had just gotten out of prison; he had just suffered persecution for His boldness in preaching the name of Jesus. Yet he was ready to take it up a notch. He said, *"Lord, please take note of their threats and grant that Your bond-servants could preach Your word with all boldness"* (Acts 4:29). He asked God to increase His boldness, which was the very thing that got him in trouble in the first place. And now he's asking for more!

We are a people chosen by God to declare what God is saying, releasing His presence over all the earth. This was all His idea—that the glory of the Lord would cover the earth as the waters cover the sea (see Hab. 2:14), and there would be no end to the increase of His government (see Isa. 9:7). You and I are servants in bringing the kingdoms of this world into His domain, where the presence of God is seen in every aspect and area of life. The Lord is looking for His Word, declared with courage, so that He *has* to show up to confirm it. May the Lord give us a word that confronts the powers of darkness, releases Heaven on earth, and launches us into our God-given destiny. That is what God will say "amen" to.

THE POWER OF RIGHTEOUSNESS

Societal transformation is not an accidental byproduct of revival. It is to be the intentional focus of a people who are filled with hope. In revival, the Church becomes more convinced of a big God than a big devil. Such a shift in focus changes what's possible. But it's our internal world that is the first thing to change in the glory of His outpouring. For such a transformation to take place in the world around us, it must first happen to the world within us. Only what is true on the inside can be released to the outside. Jesus conquered a storm with peace. It was the storm He slept in. The peace that kept Him in rest was the peace that delivered Him from the storm itself. Internal realities become our external realities when we learn to release His presence. That is the nature of ministry: Living from the inside out.

Without the outpouring of the Spirit, the Church becomes more concerned with being contaminated by evil than we are with "contaminating" the world with righteousness. While we should never take sin lightly, neither should we be ignorant of the power of holiness.

> **In revival, the Church becomes more convinced of a big God than a big devil.**

Things are different in the New Testament in that the whole covenant is given to meet the obvious need presented in the Old Testament. For example, the Gospel of Matthew was written primarily for the Jews. In this account of Jesus' life, Jesus touching the leper was the first miracle that Matthew mentioned, as it seemed to help recalibrate the reader's value system to be consistent with the value system of Jesus Himself. When He touched the leper, the leper became clean. Jesus did what was forbidden to do, bringing about what the Law was unable to do. This testimony confronted an incomplete mindset that was not adequate for His present work of grace on the earth. The power of holiness becomes even clearer when we read that a believing spouse sanctifies the entire unbelieving household. That is the power of holiness. This Kingdom mindset requires a shift in how we view and value life itself, and the effect of the life of Christ in us. Faith in Kingdom realities manifests Kingdom realities.

The power of holiness becomes clearer in the story of Daniel. God took Daniel and allowed him to be numbered with witches and warlocks before King Nebuchadnezzar. He lived righteously and brought about a New Testament effect of holiness and loyalty on an entire kingdom until that ungodly leader was converted. Holiness is more powerful than sin; it's the purity of Christ in you.

LIVING WITH HOPE

The apostle Paul demonstrates this process in Romans, which is considered the greatest theological treatise on the subject of our salvation. The first eleven chapters deal with theology and doctrine, while chapters 12 through 16 deal mostly with our conduct. A quick overview of some of the highlights in chapter 12 gives us an interesting perspective on true Kingdom attitudes that bring about change in society.

In Paul's very first statement, he declares that we are to be living offerings of worship (see Rom. 12:1). Worship is to be a primary focus that affects all we are and do. That is the context for the development of the renewed mind (see Rom. 12:2), which is absolutely essential to manifest God's Kingdom. Giving ourselves to God in worship as a living sacrifice is the context of getting our minds renewed.

He follows this with profound teaching on being faithful with our ministry gifts. In that discourse, he instructs people to prophesy *"according to their faith"* (Rom. 12:6b). This may describe why it is more common to hear words of judgment than it is to hear words of promise and hope. Our prophecies often reveal our faith.

Many prophetic words come out of human reasoning. Society always declines in the absence of revival. And the declining moral condition of the world always ends in judgment if there is no move of God. Prophetic judgments are an easy mathematical calculation. Increasing sin without repentance = judgment. That is why we are to prophesy according to faith, not human reasoning. For then we prophesy, not according to what we see in the natural, but what we see in the Spirit through faith. Note that it's the prophetic word itself that helps to bring about the change desired.

When I was a young man, the rapture of the Church was a primary subject. The return of the Lord is called *"the blessed hope"* in Scripture (Titus 2:13). But somehow we have to learn to live in a way that looks for His return without neglecting our responsibility to bring transformation to society. And whenever revival turns its focus from *being an answer to the dilemmas of life* to *heralding the return of the Lord*, the revival ends.

During those early years, many of my friends didn't go to college or pursue careers of influence because Jesus was going to return at any time. Tragically, the theology behind such an approach to life was that our beliefs contained no hope for change. We were told that things would get worse and worse until the Lord would come. Seeking change in that context wars against the very thing we were taught to hope for—His return. We were also told that there would be a great falling away and few would make it. While this kind of instruction never came from my dad, it was prevalent in the church. It became apparent to us all that it would be a waste of time to pursue positions of influence in society because Jesus was coming back at any moment. And why waste time in school when we could be involved in life now? Books were written, sermons were preached, and an appetite was created that turned our focus from the influence of the King of kings on the planet to leaving the planet to be with the King. While it was never the intention of those great authors and preachers, the hope of a generation was undermined and lost. The young men and women who would have become teachers and professors who would have been able to bring about change in an ungodly educational system from the inside chose another course of life. The lawyers and judges, politicians and business leaders were those who, for the most part, had little or no Kingdom value. The ones with the most passion chose positions of little influence. Our present chaos results in part from the errors of that era, where there was no hope for the future. And wherever hope for the future is absent, there is always a lack of prophecies that come from faith. True prophetic decrees are catalytic. They must be spoken to bring about the change they speak of. Tragically, it was during that time that abortion became legalized. Is this not a natural byproduct of not having a word of faith for tomorrow? When those left in charge, the Church, lose faith for tomorrow, we sacrifice the lives of our young.

Paul later says, *"Bless and do not curse"* in Romans 12:14. It's obvious that the believers had a tendency to curse people who were persecuting them. The lifestyles of their "enemies" brought them to such logical conclusions. Yet it is the undeserved blessing that changes the environment, making transformation possible.

The chapter ends with: *"Do not be overcome with evil, but overcome evil with good"* (Rom. 12:21). Is this not to be an action born out of the conviction that righteousness is more powerful than sinfulness? Is this not the attitude that positions us to become agents of change instead of people who want to escape? In some ways, the desire for the Lord to return right now is perhaps the most selfish desire a believer can have. Just look at the billions without Christ who would become lost forever if Jesus returned now. That must matter to us! We are the ones left on earth to intercede for their salvation. And yet that desire for His speedy return is applauded as though there were no eternal repercussions, while those who hunger for societal transformation are considered out of balance. The goodness of God demands this kind of expression from us!

Somehow we must learn how to merge the message of the *blessed hope* with that of societal transformation. We must be able to hunger for Christ and His return, yet still fully engage in our assignment to display the reality of His Kingdom now through miracles, signs, and wonders unto the transformation of cities and nations. When He asked, "Can a nation be saved in a day?" He wasn't asking for an answer. He was looking for a testimony: A generation who would bring Him the fruit of their labors—a nation. (See Isaiah 66:8.) If Jesus is the *desire of the nations*, then perhaps we, as His Body, should become desirable to the nations by becoming servants who have answers to the problems of the hour. The Church has been answering questions that the world is not asking. It's time to learn how to answer the questions they are asking so we have the favor to address the ones they should be asking. That is exactly what happened to the young man Saul. He was looking for his father's donkeys and decided to seek the counsel of the prophet Samuel. He told Saul the donkeys were found and then told him to come and see him in the morning, as he wanted to reveal the desires of his heart. Samuel answered the question he had, which positioned him to answer the question he should have been asking, which was the purpose for his life (see 1 Sam. 9:15–21).

PRAY UNTAPPED PROMISES!

There are a great number of unfulfilled prophecies that really should capture our affections and radically affect our intercessions. Here is a brief sample:

*"I will pour out My Spirit on **all** flesh"* (Joel 2:28).

*"And **all** shall know Me"* (Jeremiah 31:34; Hebrews 8:11).

*"**Many** nations shall join themselves to the Lord"* (Zechariah 2:11).

*"**Many** peoples and mighty nations will come to seek the Lord"* (Zechariah 8:22).

One of the primary responsibilities of the Church is prayer and intercession. That is part of the assignment given to priests, which is our call (see 1 Pet. 2:9). This means we are to represent people before God and contend for His mercy to be shown to the nations.

HIGHWAY OF HOLINESS

There is an environment created in the outpouring of the Spirit in which holiness becomes the normal expression of a people bathed in His presence. Isaiah speaks of this as the *highway of holiness*. A highway is a road designed to expedite travel because obstacles have been removed. It usually involves easy access and has fellow travelers. A highway of holiness allows for a momentum to be created for the people of God to live in purity effortlessly. It is so significant that even foolish things get covered. This is not to minimize sin or foolishness. It is just to help us to realize that when many live righteously, it creates a momentum where even the weak succeed.

A highway shall be there, and a road,
And it shall be called the Highway of Holiness.
The unclean shall not pass over it,
But it shall be for others.

Whoever walks the road, although a fool,

Shall not go astray (Isaiah 35:8).

This highway of holiness will not be known for compromise. There won't be people who outwardly pretend to be holy and inwardly are corrupt. *"Whoever walks the road, although a fool, shall not go astray"* (Isa. 35:8). This means that God is creating such a highway in this time of outpouring that it is going to be hard to wander off the road. This concept is difficult for many to embrace, as we are accustomed to the opposite. We have been quick to speak about the "great falling away" but not the great harvest and city transformation that is also a part of end-time prophecy. A day is coming when there will exist a righteous peer pressure, not based on punishment or the fear of man but on His manifested presence: His glory.

There is an environment created in the outpouring of the Spirit in which holiness becomes the normal expression of a people bathed in His presence.

I remember being taught that holiness is a list of things we could and could not do—and the "could not do" list was longer than the "could do" list. Mostly what was on the *can do* list was go to church, tithe, give offerings, witness, read your Bible, and pray. Then we'd throw in a potluck now and then, live a good life, and wait for Jesus to come back. But Jesus didn't go through all that He went through so we could be busy with religious activities. As meaningful as those activities can be, they are "unto" something. He placed the Spirit of the resurrected Christ within us so that we would conquer something. He is expecting fruit of the impossible from those He has empowered with the same Spirit He was empowered with, all because He is good.

New Testament theology emphasizes the power of holiness, not just the power of sin. Perhaps it is better stated that holiness is held in contrast to sin. It's not that we shouldn't fear or disregard the power of sin. Sin remains severe. But a shift in focus will prepare us to invade the world instead of requiring the world to come to us. Making this shift in perspective is essential to being positioned to bring the nations to Him. If this truth is not discovered from the heart, being salt and light serves no purpose. The salt remains in the shaker.

It is my conviction that most believers still have an Old Testament view of holiness in a New Testament era—and the eras are completely different in purpose and especially in the realm of possibilities. The Old Testament was to prepare humanity for a savior—not just to prepare them to receive one, but to prepare them to ask for one. The Law and the Prophets continually exposed requirements from God that people could not keep. But grace came along and changed everything. You can't do enough good stuff to make yourself clean before God. We are in desperate need of a savior, and even now, two thousand years later, it is vital we live with that consciousness—that we cannot work hard enough to get God's favor. We have His favor, and we must live from that favor to increase what we already have.

> The Old Testament was to prepare humanity for a savior—not just to prepare them to receive one, but to prepare them to ask for one.

One powerful concept in the Kingdom is that you get more of what you have by correctly stewarding what you have. If we can make that adjustment and learn to live in grace, our conduct changes so much more dramatically than when we try to work to obtain favor. Some of God's commands are not so much to require performance as to create correct appetites. Living out of passion is so much more Christ-like than merely living out of good discipline.

The prophet Isaiah continues with this beautiful picture of a highway for people:

> *Go through, go through the gates,*
> *Clear the way for the people;*
> *Build up, build up the highway,*
> *Remove the stones, lift up a standard over the peoples*
> (Isaiah 62:10).

I believe the gates in this passage refer to *praise*, as mentioned several verses earlier in Isaiah 60:18. When the people of God give God praise, something happens in the atmosphere. Praise in effect clears the way for people. The obstacles of impure ideologies, culture, and spiritual strongholds are confronted. Continuous praise that is both sacrificial and pure eventually removes all inferior realities, establishing a Heaven-like realm over geographical locations. It happens wherever the people of God gather to worship. But when it is sustained and pure, it eventually has an effect on entire cities. This heavenly atmosphere changes people's perception of reality. This process is called *building a highway*. A worshiping community changes the atmosphere over the city that actually creates a realm of easy access to know Christ for those who don't know Him. There is a profound connection in the unseen realm between our praises, His glory, His goodness, and the great harvest of souls. It is worthy of further study.

HOLINESS MANIFESTS IN POWER

Holiness in character is the manifestation of the power of God touching the nature of man. Holiness also affects the human body with healing. That's why it says, *"The sun of righteousness will rise with healing in its wings"* (Mal. 4:2). Holiness demands expression, and that expression is the manifestation of power. This gives language to what the Spirit of God is doing. The Lord was *"declared to be the Son of God with power according to the Spirit of holiness by the resurrection of the dead"* (Rom. 1:4). Miracles like the resurrection are a normal expression of holiness.

At times our love for God is measured by what we hate. He is still the Judge and will always condemn whatever interferes with love. How much did God hate sickness? As much as He hated sin. They are dealt with almost as one and the same. What sin is to my soul, sickness is to my body. He hated sickness enough to allow His Son to experience such a brutal beating. The blood covers our sin, but the wounds paid for our healing. That is how much He hates sin AND sickness. We cannot be tolerant of those things, because what we tolerate dominates.

OUR COMMISSION

Holiness has a transformative effect on all creation as well. Romans 8 says that *"creation groans for the revealing of the sons and daughters of God"* (Rom. 8:22). Nature longs to manifest the Kingdom. The earth groans for this, wanting to be healed. As someone recently said, even water longs to be walked on again. I'm not contending for us to try to create an earthly utopia. But I am also not discounting the fact that creation is affected by the manifestation of God's presence upon His people who have truly discovered who they are.

What happens in the spirit needs to be measurable in the natural. If you say you love God, whom you can't see, and you hate your brother, whom you can see, then what you are saying about your love for God is a lie (see 1 John 4:20). In other words, what you claim to experience in the unseen realm has to be able to be manifested in the seen realm, or what you claim is in question. He won't let us live with theories that cannot be tested. They've got to be applicable now.

The prophets used natural language to teach of spiritual realities. The desert rejoices in Isaiah 35:1. In verse 2, it blossoms abundantly with joy and singing and the glory of the Lord will be seen. Verses 3–4 are the commission: *"Strengthen weak hands. Make firm feeble knees. Say to those who are fearful hearted, 'Be strong. Do not fear. Your God will come with vengeance.'"* Run and look for anyone who's faltering and say, "This isn't the time to falter. This is our moment, the moment you were born for. Don't be afraid." Having the right message in the right hour releases an unparalleled realm of supernatural activity. This is Heaven's response to our embracing His commission: *"Then the eyes of the blind shall be opened and the ears of the deaf shall be unstopped. The lame shall leap like the deer, and the tongue of the dumb shall sing"* (Isaiah 35:5–6). This is God's "amen" to our proclaiming the right message. And he uses natural metaphor to illustrate the abundant Christian life: *"For waters will burst forth in the wilderness, and streams in the desert..."* (verse 7).

ENCOUNTERS TRANSFORM

Jesus became sin so that you and I would become the righteousness of God. We became God's righteousness in the earth. What He is changing is who we are. This transformational process through encounter continues throughout the Scripture. He says, *"Arise, shine; for your light has come,"* not "Arise and *reflect*"—because once you are touched by light (and surrender), you *become* light (Isa. 60:1). He says that if we come to Him and drink, out of our innermost being will flow rivers of living water (see John 7:38). So a drink of Him turns your innermost being into a producer of a river whose volume is so much greater than the initial drink you received. You become a releaser of that very Kingdom that impacted and changed you. Your nature, your being, your person—everything about you—is dramatically shifted in the moment you come into contact with this King and His Dominion/Kingdom.

To maintain the momentum of change, we cannot fall for distractions. And they will come. One of the main areas we are challenged in is in learning to celebrate what God celebrates.

God often hides the gifts we hunger for the most in the most unlikely packages.

We are responsible to seek Him for specific breakthroughs in private. The victories obtained in prayer become the ones displayed in public. We are also to learn from those who have already experienced the breakthrough in the areas we need. Receiving from their ministry releases a grace for us to do the same. But be ready to receive from those who are outside of your theological preferences, as God often hides the gifts we hunger for the most in the most unlikely packages. That way we will only pursue those realms in God if we have the hunger and humility to look past our differences. This way we only come into a gift we have the humility to carry faithfully. Look for the impossible and take the risks necessary to confront it and give opportunity for a miracle.

May God release a Spirit of wisdom and revelation upon His people once again so that we might see this Jesus more clearly and so that we might *re*-present this Jesus more accurately. In the same way that Moses' face shone with the glory of God after seeing His unlimited goodness, so God wants to change the face of the Church in our generation through the same revelation of His goodness. The goodness of God is the cornerstone of our theology: One that must be lived, preached, and demonstrated. It's all about Jesus. He is perfect theology.

Chapter Eleven

THE IMPORTANCE OF MYSTERY

It is not the task of Christianity to provide easy answers to every question, but to make us progressively aware of a mystery. God is not so much the object of our knowledge as the cause of our wonder.

—KALLISTOS WARE

What we don't know is sometimes as important as what we do know. While the Scriptures never exalt ignorance, they do honor trust. And trust is proven most in the midst of confusing circumstances with their corresponding questions. In effect, trust means that what we have come to know to be true about God is greater than all the circumstantial evidence that denies it. This is vital for those who display His unfolding purposes in the earth.

Remembering the purposes of God at this point is crucial. He longs to have a people who represent Jesus accurately, in purity and power, becoming those who can be trusted to co-labor with Him in a way that doesn't divide His family or pervert His reasoning. Simply put, this means to reign with Christ. His passion is to bring people into ever increasing manifestation of His presence/glory upon them. That means that the weightiness of God's glory will rest upon a people who live with an undivided heart. The bottom line is that to be a people who can carry the beauty and glory of God in the earth, we must be proven as a people of trust. And the measure of trust we live with becomes the most evident when things turn out differently than what we expected or prayed for.

BEING POWERFUL

Knowledge is power. That well-known statement is an illusion when it comes to the knowledge of God. When our knowledge of God doesn't lead us to a place of greater surrender, it leads us to greater frustration. He is predictable in that He is completely true, loving, faithful, honest, and joyfully excited about our future. He is unpredictable in that He sees the beginning from the end, and He knows the best route to take in life, even when it looks like it will turn out opposite to His promises and purposes. He will not be controlled by anyone. If you view God as your servant, He will continually frustrate you. But if you are His servant, you will constantly be in awe. It's all about perspective.

> **If you view God as your servant, He will continually frustrate you. But if you are His servant, you will constantly be in awe.**

The idea that we could ever have Him figured out gives us a false sense of control over Him, using our perception of His will to get Him to do what we want Him to do. This can become religious manipulation. He hates it and will not become subject to it.

Exposing that deception will help to keep us from becoming a people of entitlement, where we believe that God actually owes us something. Learning this area of trust will also keep us from living with the idea that we always know what's going to happen next. This is how trust is developed. And it is trust that makes us powerful.

IN LOVE WITH MYSTERY

The quote that I started with at the beginning of this chapter is one of the most meaningful quotes I have read in many years. God is more than capable of going head to head with anyone in debate. The thought that God might be intimidated with humanity's questions is quite humorous. He invites us into this dialogue. (See Isaiah 1:18.) It's just that He has a different value system than we do, although ours is changing daily in our walk with Him. And to have a relationship with Him is always on His terms. But we know that His terms are always for our best. God has one basic requirement of anyone who approaches Him—faith. *"Without faith it is impossible to please Him"* (Heb. 11:6). That is what He values.

> **Bold faith stands on the shoulders of quiet trust.**

Living in the place of trust positions us for breakthroughs—bold faith stands on the shoulders of quiet trust. Faith is an activity of the heart. Real faith comes through yieldedness, not some trumped-up activity of the brain. Faith comes from surrender, not striving. Faith is not mindless. Understanding with the renewed mind (see Rom. 12:2) can often be used to set the context for faith to work in, much like the banks of a river set the parameters for the flow of the water. While faith is not mindless, it is also not mind-full. It is not intellectual in nature. True faith is superior to reason in that it gives our intellect a context in which to grow safely—in the knowledge of God. Remember, it's the fool who says in His heart there is no God. (See Psalm 14:1; 53:1.) The Eternal God is the cornerstone of all logic and reason.

God cannot be comprehended. If it were possible, we, not He, would be God—the finite will never envelop the infinite. He is to be known by relationship. Consider the wonder of the Almighty God even wanting for us to know Him. Because Jesus took our sins upon Himself, we are authorized to approach the Father with the same qualifications that Jesus has in coming before His Father. Jesus is received and celebrated by a perfect Father who is always good. Every true believer is equally received and celebrated because we are in Christ.

To know God is the greatest privilege given to anyone. The cross of Jesus Christ is the ultimate invitation to know God. It is here we can know with certainty He has spared no expense in enabling us to respond successfully to His invitation.

Clarity on this mystery of head vs. heart is given in Ephesians 3:19. It says, *"to know the love of Christ which passes knowledge; that you may be filled with all the fullness of God."* The word *know* is a word that means "knowledge gained through experience." It is experiential knowledge. The word *knowledge* means "to comprehend." In so many words Paul is saying, *that we might know the love of God by experience in a way we could never comprehend or fully understand.* It's not that knowledge is wrong, or that ignorance is exalted. Knowledge is vital. We have teachers in the Body of Christ so we will learn. In fact, one of the main responsibilities of the Holy Spirit is to teach us—it's a divine priority. But we must require of our own hearts that the knowledge of Him takes us to Him. Through an encounter with God, we grow in divine wisdom. It's that knowledge is not required for faith.

My Dad

My dad was such a wonderful man. He was a great spiritual leader who loved people so profoundly. He is considered a hero of the faith for many, as their lives were eternally changed through his loving care. There are also many people who serve in the ministry of the Gospel today, all over the world, who credit my dad with being the encouragement that helped them get to their place of service. He had a knack for spotting the ones who were different and as such may not have met all the requirements for the position they pursued—too young, too old, too broken of a background, too many children, too bold, makes too many messes, and on and on. But he especially loved those. He saw something in them that made him stand out among his peers. I called him a Barnabas. Barnabas's name means *son of encouragement*. Barnabas did that exact thing with a guy the entire Church was afraid of—Saul of Tarsus, who became the apostle Paul. Only the Lord knows what would have happened to this guy who was known for his messes had not Barnabas adopted him and brought him into his circle of encouragement. That was my dad. And he truly was the greatest encouragement of my life.

He served in our denomination for many years in a high official capacity. I remember when he left the position he loved so much. He wanted to be with family, but he also wanted to be in a place where God could be God, doing what He wanted to do, and not be controlled by well-meaning church leaders. He was a great lover of revival and wanted to participate in one yet again. He loved what we were experiencing at Bethel Church in Redding, California. The presence and power of the Holy Spirit that we had come to witness was very similar to what he grew up with. As a result, he moved to Redding to help us in whatever capacity would best serve this wonderful move of God. The wisdom and encouragement that poured from him helped us in ways that will only be measurable in eternity. I'm so thankful for those days.

I was ministering in Brazil with one of my best friends, Randy Clark. I received an urgent phone call, giving me the most unexpected news: That they had just found pancreatic cancer in my dad. What a shock! He went in for a simple procedure with his gall bladder, but none of us expected anything of this magnitude. I had to go home immediately. Randy released me from my responsibilities for the remainder of the trip, and I flew home. It was time for a miracle.

Cancer had become a very specific target for us. I hear far too many Christians mention the word *cancer* almost with a reverence. To recognize it as a powerful entity is costly. It would be like Israel respecting Baal, or some other false deity. The spirit behind such diseases can recognize our fear. Cancer, and every other disease, is an inferior name to the name of Jesus. It must bow. None of us should have any respect for that disease. (I don't mean respect in the sense of honor. I know of no one who does that. I mean respect by the place of "awe" it has obtained in the hearts and minds of God's people.) Cancer has become the Goliath of the New Testament Church in North America. We must do what David did and run toward the giant to see it killed! (See 1 Samuel 17.) It is inexcusable to withdraw in reverence, as did Saul and his armies when Goliath taunted the armies of God. We are the most to be pitied when the size of our God (in our eyes) is smaller than the size of our problem. We must return to Big God, little devil.

I returned home with the resolve to see cancer bow its knee once again. We have seen thousands of people healed of all sorts of problems, including many with cancer. This would be one more occasion to see the name of Jesus exalted and another point of celebration for my family—both natural and spiritual. Upon my arrival, I went immediately to see him and to pray. I continued with frequent visits and prayers, as did many others from our staff and church family. The prayer times were powerful with a great sense of God's presence.

The full story isn't necessary here at this point. What is important for you to know is that he lived only six more months. The loss was painful, really painful. And to be honest, it still is. He was seventy-five years old, which I guess seems old enough to many. But both sides of my family live well into their eighties—the youngest to die before him that I can recall was eighty-six. His mother lived to be ninety-seven. And my dad had been the healthiest of them all. I thought he would be with us for at least another ten years, if not twenty. It didn't work out that way. For what it's worth, we also don't think it's necessary to die of a sickness that Jesus defeated. It's a wrong way of thinking to assume that we must die by disease. Yet he did.

Most of our immediate family was present in his bedroom when my dad went to be with the Lord. I forget exactly how many it was, but it was somewhere between twenty and thirty people, including grandchildren. We surrounded his bed, singing, praying, laughing, telling stories, and just being family. It was important for him, as well as the rest of us. Both he and my mom had built the legacy of this family to be together in joy and in pain. When he breathed his last, a gasp filled the room. It was like someone punched us in the gut collectively. After perhaps five minutes had passed, I asked the entire family to gather around his bed. We sang a song of praise, exalting God for His goodness. I think we all knew that we would not have the chance to give God that particular offering in Heaven—there's no pain, confusion, disappointment, grief, disillusionment, or any such thing in Heaven. Those are the experiences we have in this life, and I didn't want us to miss our opportunity to give Him this costly sacrifice of praise when it seemed most unreasonable. And so we did. We honored God for His goodness and His promise to heal. It was a sacrifice. But it will never be one I regretted giving Him.

My dad was known for so many things. But I think one of the most profound areas of his impact was that he was a worshiper. Both he and my mom carried that assignment and privilege so well. They modeled *the heart of a worshiper* for the rest of us. And while we were already a family dedicated to honor God with thanksgiving, praise, and worship, we realized there was now a mantle of responsibility to maintain and build upon the foundation he laid. I spoke to the family about his "mantle" for worship and how it was now our responsibility to pick it up. We made a covenant before God to be faithful to our tribal call. It was beautiful and tender. We took some time to say "yes" to God and give praise for His goodness.

ENDURING FAITH

The two most difficult messages I've ever preached were the Sunday before he died and the Sunday after. I entitled those two messages "Enduring Faith." I've had more feedback from those two messages than any others in my forty-plus years of ministry. They were honest and filled with both grief and hope. Faith doesn't deny a problem's existence. It just denies it a place of influence. The messages basically came down to this—I don't have the right to adjust my *assignment from God* to what I think I am qualified for or can do well. He told us to pray for the sick. It was His idea. It must not diminish because of this loss, nor can we afford to create a theology based on what didn't happen. By setting the boy free, Jesus refused to allow His disciples to create theology around the absence of deliverance of the child in Mark 9.

> **Faith doesn't deny a problem's existence. It just denies it a place of influence.**

LIVING OUT LOUD

Although I'm a rather private person by nature, I could sense it was important to live my loss in the open so we could learn together as a church family. That's a very vulnerable place to be in, because you don't know what the outcome will be. But we did know that God was good and still in charge. So we processed it out loud, together, in worship, and in the celebration of God's goodness. We learned together, largely of the peace that passes understanding. You don't get the peace that passes understanding until you give up your right to understand. We learned that no question has the power to undermine what God has already shown us, unless we give it that power. And finally we learned it's OK not to have answers for questions. In fact, it

> **You don't get the peace that passes understanding until you give up your right to understand.**

was not only acceptable; we learned it was one of the most beautiful and important positions to be in as a family of believers.

God is attracted to weakness and brokenness, and that was the condition of our hearts. Not broken and depressed—not broken because of being stiff-necked in resistance to God—broken because of tenderness to the only One with the right to rule over our lives. We said yes to Him long before we knew what the outcome would be. And in that place of "yes!" we found that this Father, who is good beyond measure, came and brought healing to our brokenness. The outcome is strength, peace, and breakthrough.

THE BEAUTY OF VINDICATION

I had a conversation with Rick Joyner on the phone a couple of days before my dad's death. He told me that this loss would give me access to a seven times greater anointing against this particular disease. That may sound a bit awkward to some, but I knew of the principle first established by Solomon in Proverbs 6:30–31: *"People do not despise a thief if he steals to satisfy himself when he is starving. Yet when he is found, he must restore sevenfold; he may have to give up all the substance of his house."* The devil is called the thief, and he stole from our family. I also knew that greater anointing was not to be given automatically. It would require time in the *secret place*, crying out for the more that God had promised. It was not begging, in the sense of there being a fear God wouldn't keep His promise. I just knew that not everything was automatic. Sometimes He waits to see if the promise will awaken something in us that can carry the weightiness of the answer we've asked for. When answers to prayer come to a yielded heart, they release greater strength. But when answers come to a resistant heart, they carry a high probability of deepening the independence that causes conflict with God in the first place. The recalibration of our value system needed to be consistent with His.

The Book of First Samuel has a story that becomes vital for us in this journey. There is a woman named Hannah, who was barren. And while she was loved much by her husband, she was not fulfilled in life without a child. At the same time, we find Israel was in trouble again, and God desired a solution—He wanted them to have a trustworthy prophet. Hannah became so desperate in her prayers that she promised God that if He would bless her with a son, she would return the child to God, dedicating him to a life of ministry. Without knowing it, she aligned her heart's cry for a son with God's heart cry for a prophet. It was when both worlds came into agreement that we see Heaven invade earth, giving her the son she longed for. She went on to have many more children, as God honored her sacrifice of heart to meet the longing He had for Israel to have a trusted voice from God.

I do believe God hates cancer and that He wants His people to rise up with His hatred toward that disease. But hate it enough to seek God in private and take risk in public. As I've stated before, there are times when our love for God can be measured by what we hate. And in this case, hate what He hates—disease.

How do you think our perfect Father feels about sickness and disease? It was the burden of all of humanity's afflictions for all time that was put upon His Son, Jesus Christ. He bore our sickness upon His body in His suffering so we could be healed. How should a Father feel toward a disease that has such a painful impact on His Son? That is how we are to feel. We must hate what He hates and love what He loves.

JOHN THE BAPTIST

One day, while John was baptizing people in the river, he noticed a man in the distance. He pointed to Him, saying, "Look, the Lamb of God, who takes away the sins of the world" (see John 1:29). John had prophesied of His coming. But now He is present.

If we fast-forward John's story, we find him in prison, about to die. He is now in a completely different frame of mind. As a result, He sends a couple of his disciples to Jesus asking if He is the *Coming One* or not. That is an interesting question to be asking the One you've already announced as *the* One everyone was looking for.

I remind you, John is in prison, and his assignment was to be a voice in the wilderness. Part of his assignment was to prepare the way for the One who releases from prison. (See Luke 4:18.) John had the sense that he wasn't going to get out. How would it feel to prepare the way for the One who would be known for releasing prisoners, but you wouldn't be one of them? Perhaps that's why John is asking the question—he wanted to make sure he got it right. Jesus' answer is a lesson in itself. He told John's disciples to tell John what they'd seen and heard. (See Matthew 11.) Jesus could have given John a verse-by-verse study of the prophets to prove His identity. He easily could have taken John through the story of the manger, the announcement of the angels, the shepherds, and the wise men. Instead He points to what He is doing—miracles. That is not a statement against the study of Scripture. It's a simple acknowledgment of the tool that Jesus used. Perhaps John's attention was on what God wasn't doing—releasing him from prison. Jesus, wanting John's life to end well, turned his attention back to what He was doing—bringing healing, deliverance, and declaring the Good News. It is dangerous to form a belief system around what we don't see happening in our lives. That is an experience-based theology, not a Scripture-based theology.

My dad didn't get healed. He is in Heaven. Let's be honest, this whole situation is a win-win for the believer. I just don't want to be found expecting something (death, loss, and destruction—John 10:10) that Jesus never once expected, taught, or modeled for us. Jesus did not teach us how to live without miracles. It wasn't His experience, nor is it to be ours.

LIVING BETWEEN TWO WORLDS

Eternity runs through our veins, yet we live in time. We are citizens of earth, but we are already citizens of Heaven. We are saved, yet we will be saved when Jesus comes for us. Our old nature has been crucified with Christ, yet our capacity to sin has not disappeared. We are introduced to a kingdom that is both here and now, yet this very same kingdom is coming. We often live in tension, often between two conflicting realities. That is the life of a believer. And that is why the life of trust is to be built, not upon principles or theories, but upon the solid rock called God's goodness. Sometimes the conflict in our souls, or the confusion in our minds, is to bring us face to face with that which is the most reliable and dependable—the goodness of God. The psalmist knew this exact truth when confronted with adversaries and false witnesses threatening violence upon him. His response must become our response, regardless of what the devil throws our way: *"I would have lost heart, unless I had believed that I would see the goodness of the Lord in the land of the living"* (Ps. 27:13).

BECAUSE OF TRUST

The need for mystery need not be painful or dreaded. It is a part of our ongoing story. We value the outcome—the miracles, the breakthroughs, and the divine interventions—as we should. But He seems to treasure the process—that which takes us to the outcome. It's the process that reveals and demonstrates our devotion to Him. Devotion, that realm of established trust, is something He can build upon. God is the ultimate entrepreneur, building the unexpected in the earth upon and through the lives of His trusted saints.

What we really believe about Him becomes evident in trial. Answers to prayers are the easiest things in the world for God. He is all-powerful. What He doesn't control is our response to Him. He has influence, but not control, as He has given us a most valuable gift—a free will. When our will is surrendered to His purposes, all of creation gets closer to the healing God promised, as His people find out who they are. (See Romans 8:19.) We are to reign with Christ. It's vital to see this destiny in the way it was presented to us, as our beloved King put a towel over His arm and washed His disciples' feet. He rules to serve. Our privilege in life is to serve with the heart of a king and rule with the heart of a servant. Reigning with

Christ will never equip us to exercise power over people but instead will allow us the opportunity to serve sacrificially—following the example given to us by Jesus.

One of the great Old Testament statements will serve us well at this point. It's wisdom to realize what God has given us access to and what is to remain entirely in His possession. This is where trust is proven.

> *The secret things belong to the Lord our God, but those things which are revealed belong to us and to our children forever, that we may do all the words of this law* (Deuteronomy 29:29).

I believe in miracles and have seen more than I ever even hoped to see as a young man. My experience has been what Jesus promised—the blind see, the deaf hear, the lame walk, and the poor have the Good News declared to them. My conclusion is miracles happen entirely by His grace. I've seen them happen when there was great faith, as well as when there was simple obedience in prayer but no real expectation of a miracle. It's still all by grace. And while this life of following Jesus is to be a life filled with supernatural interventions, we are given the following passage for a reason: *"And we know that all things work together for good to those who love God, to those who are the called according to His purpose"* (Rom. 8:28). Such a promise would never be necessary if everything worked the way we expected. God is not a vending machine where we put in a coin and pull the handle and get what we requested. He is a Father that is to be known. Trusting Him enough to embrace mystery as a gift is one of the quickest ways to come to know this One who is beyond knowing, whose ways are always good.

I grew up in an athletic home and have always been very involved in sports. Most of my involvement now in sports is in watching my grandchildren. It's so fun. Beni and I also have our favorite professional teams in baseball, football, and basketball. We love to watch our teams play on TV, rooting, sometimes loudly, from our family room. Occasional shouts of joy are heard when our team does well, as well as deep groans of travail when they've done poorly. Our schedule doesn't always allow us to watch games live. Thankfully, we're able to record them and watch them at a later time. Beni and I are much different in our approach in watching a recorded game. She doesn't want to know the outcome of the game before watching. She loves the process of the game, enjoying it as though it were live. I, on the other hand, want to know the outcome before I sit down to watch it. If my team lost, I usually won't watch the game. While there is a good reason for both approaches, mine gives me an advantage that fits well in this subject of mystery. If my favorite pitcher gives up a homerun in the first inning of the game, or my team's quarterback throws an interception on the opening drive, I already know it doesn't change the outcome because my team has already won the game. There's very little stress, if any, when I see my team make an error in baseball, or fumble the ball in football. Why? I know the outcome. The one thing we're assured of in walking with the Lord is the outcome. He has already recorded the score of the game in His book of records, and we win! Because of this, adversity, conflict, or problems need not lead to panic or despair. I know ahead of time how it turns out. *All things work together for good*" (Rom. 8:28)! Because of this, I can legitimately give Him an offering of thanks for what I need before it has actually taken place, for in His book the score is already recorded. Knowing how things will turn out based on the promises of a good and perfect Father changes the nature of every day of my life.

Chapter Twelve

NOW WHAT?

Jesus's resurrection is the beginning of God's new project not to snatch people away from earth to heaven but to colonize earth with the life of heaven. That, after all, is what the Lord's Prayer is about.

—N.T. WRIGHT

God's goodness is bigger and more valuable than creation itself. It is the most unexplored reality in existence. It is too great a reality to look at passively as an add-on to the faith. This that is greater than space and time must be embraced with hearts of surrender, with bold and courageous hearts of surrender. The level of deception even in the hearts of God's people has been so strong that there is an arrogance masquerading as humility teaching us to receive the evil that comes our way as the mysterious hand of God. It's arrogance because it comes from the soulish ideals of people without biblical roots, without biblical surrender. Yielding to God's goodness should be easier than it is. Yet it has become the challenge of the hour—because this surrender is so entirely a grace expression of Heaven that no one could ever take the credit for what God has done in us.

I've heard mountain climbers questioned in interviews as to why they climb a particular mountain. The common answer is, "Because it's there." In other words, the very presence of a seemingly impossible task itself is an invitation to explore and conquer. And while the goodness of God will never be conquered, in the sense of comprehended or controlled, it must be explored. Its very existence is the overwhelming invitation. *"For the word of the Lord is right, and all His work is done in truth. He loves righteousness and justice; the earth is full of the goodness of the Lord"* (Ps. 33:4–5). One of the definitions for this word *full* is "having no empty space." It's beautiful. The world has no empty spaces untouched by God's goodness.

> **God's goodness is bigger and more valuable than creation itself. It is the most unexplored reality in existence.**

That being the case, no one has to look far to find this treasure. But one may have to look differently.

I have a responsibility to steward the knowledge of His goodness. If in fact all of this is true, then my thoughts must be consistent with this reality. I am the one that must change. I must think consistently with who He is and what He is like, or I will feed my soul on the inferior, living with the assumption that what I think I know is true. One of the great tragedies in life is to spend great amounts of time and energy believing something and then finding out it's not true. Anchoring our souls in everything but His goodness is the ultimate waste of time.

Moses made a stunning request in His pursuit of the *more of God*: *"Let me know Your ways that I may know You"* (Ex. 33:13).

Discovering what He is like is the invitation of God to deepen the relationship with God. In other words, because the relationship with God is built upon His goodness, that very discovery affords us the opportunity to take greater and greater risks to pursue the abundance that is God Himself, for He is faithful and true.

I'M IN DEBT

I live with the conviction that I am in debt to this world. I'm not talking about being in debt financially. I'm referring to the simple realization that unless certain realities are active in my life, those around me may never discover who they are or why they're alive. I/we play a role in this transaction. When those realities are alive and well in me, God becomes the overwhelming treasure for life. Mark Twain said that the two most important days in a person's life are the day he is born and the day he finds out why. That's a great statement. We can contribute to that discovery by taking responsibility for what God made possible for us through the Gospel of good news.

> I must think consistently with who He is and what He is like, or I will feed my soul on the inferior, living with the assumption that what I think I know is true.

Having said that, here are three areas that I believe I owe the world:

1. An encounter with God.

2. An example.

3. A message of good news.

A GOD ENCOUNTER

Living a life filled with the Spirit of God is the only possible way I can consistently bring others into an encounter with God. Maintaining an awareness of Him, with the willingness to do whatever He wants, makes this challenging goal doable.

Oftentimes, people travel great distances to come to Redding to receive a miracle. I'm thankful for all that God has done and for the countless numbers of people who have been healed or delivered. At the end of a Sunday morning service, I go to the back door to bless the people as they leave. It's a great moment for me as I get to connect with the people I love, even though it's brief. Oftentimes, a line forms to the side of people who are waiting for me to pray for them. Usually the line is made up of people who need a miracle. And while we have teams of people that serve following every service who are trained for this purpose, some will come to me thinking I have a greater anointing for healing than the others. That isn't true. But when someone is in pain or dying, that is not the time for a theological discussion. So I pray. It's so wonderful when Jesus comes and brings a miracle. I rejoice with the person and give God the glory. But more often than I care to admit, the person leaves with no noticeable change. When I get alone with the Lord, I pray, *"Father, that person came a great distance hoping to meet with You, and all they met was me. And neither of us was impressed. You've got to do something in my life so deeply that when people come to me, they encounter You."* That prayer is an ongoing cry.

To illustrate what it looks like to be full of the Holy Spirit, I often take an unopened water bottle. I then ask the question, "Is this water bottle full?" And of course, the answer is "yes." It is full by the acceptable standards set by the manufacturer. But it isn't really full, at least not as full as it could be. I then open the bottle and pour into it from another bottle until it overflows. Everybody seems to get the illustration quickly. It is only full when it is over-flowing—fullness is measured in the overflow. It's the same for us. Being filled with the Spirit does not point to an experience we might have had a certain number of years ago. It's not measured by what I contain but by what flows from me. Only in the continual overflow of His presence through our lives are we truly full of the Holy Spirit. And it's in that condition that we are most likely able to bring others into an encounter with God.

The concept of His flowing from us might be a little abstract for some. But the idea has its roots in Jesus' teaching to His disciples. In John 7:38–39, Jesus said, *"He who believes in Me, as the Scripture said, 'From his innermost being will flow rivers of living water.' But this He spoke of the Spirit."* The picture He gives us in this passage is profound. He is teaching us what happens when we minister in His anointing—what happens when God has His way through us. It's like a river flowing from us. And that river is the Holy Spirit. It couldn't be clearer. He flows from us. And this time, the picture is not of a water bottle to contain Him. He is in us as a river to impact the spiritual geography around us. He lives in us, but He wants out—He is in us as a river, not a lake. He is a flowing presence, carrying the heart of the Father, desiring to saturate the land with the works of Jesus.

AN EXAMPLE

People need mentors and models to illustrate how to do life. It's so much quicker to learn from someone who is farther down the road than we are. The Bible calls it being a disciple, which means *learner.* And while the concept of discipleship is included in this point, being *an example* is much bigger than that. It is more about *who we are* because we have discovered the One who is good than *what we can do* because we've developed a spiritual skill. Because He is a good and perfect Father, I must dream accordingly—consistent with His nature and promises.

Jesus introduced the subject of a good God giving good gifts as only a perfect Father could do. (See Matthew 7:11.) In that passage, Jesus asked, *"How much more"* referring to the Father giving us better gifts than we have the character or resources to match. The illustration is an invitation for us to dream—to dream as a child.

I have three children, each with amazing spouses, who have given Beni and me nine grandchildren. I can't imagine being more blessed than I am. All fifteen of them are the absolute delight of our lives.

> Being filled with the Spirit does not point to an experience we might have had a certain number of years ago. It's not measured by what I contain but by what flows from me.

It seems like all the children in our world wear capes when they're young—Superman, Batman, Wonder Woman, and the like. It's so much fun to watch them dream and play. This is such a precious time in life when they think they are so much bigger than they really are. Recently, at one of my grandson's T-Ball games (a form of baseball fitting for a five-year-old), he told his dad that he should get off the field because he might get hurt. He was pretty certain he needed to protect his dad and that he was big enough to do it. It's cute and fun to watch them exercise their identity muscles. People who are able to keep alive the child-like approach to life, especially the ability to dream, have much better self-esteem and generally accomplish more than those who were told not to dream so big.

Tragically, our educational system often kills a child's capacity to dream, attempting to bring conformity. Parents often contribute to this malady of the soul in attempts to keep the child from dis-appointment. Their thinking is, *How many presidents of the US can there be?* or *There are only so many astronauts in the world. The odds aren't really high that my child will be one of them* or *Very few actually make it into the world of professional sports.* The fear of dis-appointment has become for some worse than the disappointment itself. Yet failed attempts are so much better than no attempts at all. Dreaming well exercises a muscle of the inner person that will pay off sooner or later.

We are to become a people for whom God loves to fulfill dreams. That blessing of God's favor upon us is to display God's nature in such a wonderful way that even nations will be attracted to God. That is the rather stunning theme of the entire 67th psalm. *"That Your way may be known on the earth, Your salvation among all nations"* (verse 2). And while I referred to this psalm earlier in the book, this truth fits perfectly in this concluding chapter. The revelation of God's nature (His goodness) brings the nations to Him. But His nature is seen in His blessing upon His children. I do believe that the blessing of God upon us is connected deeply to His fulfilling the dreams of our hearts. Those dreams will always reveal our own unique expression of His purposes being fulfilled in and through our lives. This beautiful manifestation of being co-laborers, dream-ing like the original dreamer, is not a threat to God anymore than it is for any of us as parents to see our own children fulfill their dreams and purpose in life. In fact, it could be said that fulfill-ing our dreams in life is a fulfillment of His dream—a people like His Son in character, lifestyle, and heart. God's delight in our lib-erty and freedom, coupled with our own uniqueness, is beyond our ability to comprehend. I often tell people that if they knew who God created them to be, they would never want to be anyone else! This is His heart for people. Religion, which is form without power, does the opposite. It kills, smothers, and controls. That's why our discovery of the goodness of God is to become an overwhelming breakthrough for all of us, so that our influence in this world is not based on ideals, concepts, or principles alone. Instead, it is based on a life of enviable freedom. I remind you that the works of the Lord in Acts 14:17 are His calling card, left in our lives as a witness of His nature. In the same way, our liberty becomes *the calling card of God* that gives witness to the nature of our Father in people's lives. As you can imagine, this must be visible. It can't just be a doctrine or a discipline. While those things are vital, His blessings must be measureable to have effect in this world.

The Power of Wisdom

The word for *proverb* comes from a word that means "to reign." Brian Simmons, in his wonderful Passion Translation, points out what might be key to grasping the Book of Proverbs and its ultimate purpose. It comes down to this—wisdom is to enable us to reign in life. That doesn't mean to reign over people. Wisdom does little to help the power-hungry person. Instead, it shows us how Jesus Christ, the person called Wisdom (see 1 Cor. 1:30), lived in such triumph and victory as the Son of Man. To reign in life means money doesn't rule me. I reign over money, using it as the tool that God intended, without falling into the trap of trying to measure my spirituality by what I own. Reigning in life means that I am not controlled by the fear of man, but instead I live in the fear of God. Circumstances don't run my life. I reign over circumstances. Reigning in life means I live with the tools to have a healthy family. This is the role and benefit of wisdom. This wisdom enables us to model a life of victory that has the potential to attract those whose lives are ruled by all these little foxes that spoil the vineyards of their lives. Wisdom puts us in a place to bring others into our personal victory.

Becoming Like Jesus

If you thought becoming like Jesus just means when He walked the earth in purity and power, you might have a surprise coming. The apostle John walked with Jesus during His earthly ministry and was with Him at the Last Supper. And then He saw Him in Revelation 1:13–17. This time He was completely different from before.

> *I saw one like a son of man, clothed in a robe reaching to the feet, and girded across His chest with a golden sash. His head and His hair were white like white wool, like snow; and His eyes were like a flame of fire. His feet were like burnished bronze, when it has been made to glow in a furnace, and His voice was like the sound of many waters. In His right hand He held seven stars, and out of His mouth came a sharp two-edged sword; and His face was like the sun shining in its strength. When I saw Him, I fell at His feet like a dead man.*

This same apostle John made the most astonishing statement of all regarding our identity and likeness. He said, *"As He is, so also are we in this world"* (1 John 4:17). We are actually being transformed into the likeness of Jesus in His resurrected, ascended, and glorified state. I'll admit, that statement might be the biggest stretch of all on both our minds and our faith—infinitely beyond comprehension.

So, how and where is Jesus right now? He is seated on the throne in Heaven, at the right hand of the Father, filled with and emanating His glory, interceding for us. There it is! We are *seated* in heavenly places in Christ (see Eph. 2:6), reigning with Him. The Scripture says, *"Christ in you, the hope of glory,"* which tells us plainly that any chance of the glory of God being manifest in and through us will be according to the reality of Jesus Christ abiding in us (Col. 1:27). And then finally, just as He is interceding for us, so we, too, must pray for the mercy of God to be extended to others in the same way it was given to us. (See Romans 8:34.)

Our lives are not being conformed into the image of the One headed to the cross, as wonderful as that was. Instead, we are being transformed into the likeness of the One who has been raised from the dead, has ascended to the right hand of the Father, and is glorified before all things in Heaven and on earth.

We are to provide an example for people to follow through purity, power, and presence. These influences change everything.

THE MESSAGE

I owe people the message of the Gospel of the Kingdom of God. It must be declared. This wonderful message includes the good news of salvation for lost and broken humanity, which is all of us. But it is much bigger than that. It is the proclamation of God's rule over everything that exists, in the natural realm as well as the spiritual. And all of that is in the *here and now*. Whatever He rules over has life, freedom, beauty, and order. The decree itself is important because some things don't manifest until they are spoken. If we realized how what we say attracts spiritual reinforcements, angelic or demonic, we'd be much more careful to watch what we say. We'd also be more deliberate in proclaiming what is true—God is in charge and longs to manifest His goodness everywhere.

We sometimes make the mistake of thinking that if we believe the right things, then everything will work out fine. While right beliefs are essential, there is more. So many of the breakthroughs in Scripture would not have happened if the people hadn't declared what God told them to declare. Jesus told us, *"Whoever says to this mountain, 'Be taken up and cast into the sea,' and does not doubt in his heart, but believes that what he says is going to happen, it will be granted him"* (Mark 11:23). The concept taught here by Jesus is modeled in both the Old and New Testaments. Bold declarations are important. (I realize that the principles of confession and decree have been misused. But the idea of avoiding this truth because of others' errors is akin to refusing to use any currency because counterfeits exist. Misuse by others does not justify no use by me.)

It is good news. It must be preached. *"How then will they call on Him in whom they have not believed? How will they believe in Him whom they have not heard? And how will they hear without a preacher?"* (Rom. 10:14). The message of the Kingdom is received with repentance. People must turn from their sin and put their faith in the Son of God. Treating sin lightly doesn't help the people we're serving. Confession of sin is coming into agreement with God about our need for forgiveness and our hopeless condition apart from Jesus. Because repentance means to change the way we think, the sorrow for sin must be deep enough to provoke an inward change in our perspective on reality. We must keep it real.

The message of the Kingdom is what Jesus preached, and to illustrate that it was for His followers, too, Paul preached it. At the end of the Book of Acts, we have the following statement that summarizes the message of this apostle's life: *"And he stayed two full years in his own rented quarters and was welcoming all who came to him, preaching the kingdom of God and teaching concerning the Lord Jesus Christ with all openness, unhindered"* (Acts 28:30–31).

Boldness in preaching this message attracts Heaven. The record of Scripture demonstrates how God responds to the bold declaration of the Gospel. (See Acts 4:28–29.) It's beautiful. But still many don't take this mandate seriously because the message of God ruling over us seems so invasive. In this case, we, the messengers, must repent before we can expect the people to repent. It's wrong thinking that must change.

The concept of ruling is offensive because of the abuses of power-hungry people. But abusive people do not illustrate or define God. They rule for their own benefit as they rule out of fear instead of love. If we understood the goodness of God, this subject of a King who rules over us would bring great joy to our hearts. He is the model for all government, displaying His two basic purposes—ruling and serving. Those principles apply to all rulership, whether it's over a nation, business, home, or whatever. First we *rule to protect*, and second we *serve to empower*. Peter gives us the following charge: *"Submit yourselves for the Lord's sake to every human institution, whether to a king as the one in authority, or to governors as sent by Him for the punishment of evildoers and the praise of those who do right"* (1 Pet. 2:13–14). The *punishment of evildoers* is the protection part of this equation. *Punishment* brings justice and restitution to the victim, creating boundaries for ongoing protection. The *praise of those who do right* is the empowering part of governing. Leading this way gives attention to what you want to increase in the land, if you're a political leader, and in your home, if you're a parent. The honor that comes from leaders goes a long way in establishing the grounds for promotion and increases as a healthy part of our culture. Deep personal fulfillment comes to everyone when there is this kind of righteous leadership. These two elements are to be the main responsibilities of all government, with the Kingdom of God being the ultimate example. For this reason, our message of *"the Kingdom of God is at hand"* is to bring great delight because we know the liberty it brings (Mark 1:15). We also know that Jesus is the desire of all nations. (See Haggai 2:7.) That being said, the bold declaration of this message brings the only possible solution to the inward cry of everyone we know.

THE HEART OF GOD

One of the more shocking discoveries for us has been that God is actually in a good mood. He sees the beginning from the end and is convinced that His plan of redeeming people from their sin, enabling them to rule with Christ, will actually work. He has given us His best—Jesus, the Son of God, and the Holy Spirit—to live in us. In some ways, this statement of God's mood is one of the more alarming statements for many, especially for those who view Him as constantly on the verge of an angry outburst of some sort. My main goal is to at least make people think of how we perceive Him. Because He is better than we think, let's change the way we think and let the whole world know He really is in a good mood.

Chapter Thirteen

GOD'S GOODNESS
EXPRESSED IN HONOR

Jesus chased the moneychangers out of the temple with a whip. He confronted Pharisees often, refusing to give in to their strange ideas of ministry and their complete lack of value for those bound by sin. He revealed the heart of the Father accurately in every encounter He had, including during times of great conflict. His love for the Father enabled Him to see and do what only He was doing (see John 5:19). His high value for people was especially evident for those who didn't know they had any worth. Zeal for His house consumed Him. Remember, His house is people (see John 2:17; Eph. 2:21–22). It would do us all some good to examine the variety of ways He responded to people in different situations.

The culture of honor has become a popular subject in recent days, and for good reason. It is the biblical posture needed to effectively disciple nations, as it reveals the heart of a good Father. The culture of honor is not in conflict with a bold and aggressive approach to ministry. It is the overall attitude of the heart that Jesus set for

217

us. But it works best in the atmosphere of honest communication, which sometimes requires boldness. The bottom line is, we have the privilege to live honorably.

BOLDNESS NEED NOT BE HARSH

My early years in Christ were steeped in strong discipleship in which it became our joy to lay down our lives for Jesus. It was an all-or-nothing approach to following Jesus that remains the standard for me to this day. I'm so thankful that such training is in my spiritual upbringing. But more than a few of us also picked up a harshness toward others in our efforts to follow Christ without compromise. With that as my lens, it was hard to see the tenderness of Jesus in Scripture and especially hard to see Him honor people. Yet He did.

When we have that attitude, it is way too easy to interpret His actions through our values and lifestyle, instead of having our lifestyle influenced by His. Jesus brought honor to people whom most of us never would have honored. The results were quite astounding.

HIS KINDNESS LEADS US

One of my favorite stories in this regard is found in Luke 5. Peter had already fished all night and had nothing to show for his labors. Jesus came upon the scene after Peter had returned to shore with an unsuccessful night behind him. Jesus told him to put out into the deep and let down his nets for a catch—something he had done all night long. Peter's response was brilliant: *"Master, we worked hard all night and caught nothing, but I will do as You say and let down the nets"* (Luke 5:5 NASB). When he did, they caught such a large amount of fish that the boat began to sink. Peter called for his partners in the other boat to come and help. They did, and their boat began to sink as well. The catch was so large that it left a profound mark on the thinking of the entire group of disciples involved in that business. This was especially true after Jesus then told them His purpose: *"Do not fear, from now on you will be catching men"* (Luke 5:10 NASB). This is an amazing story for so many reasons, not the least of which is Jesus' idea of the harvest of souls. The abundance of fish was to be forever etched in their minds as the model for what they should expect in their ministry to the lost—an abundance in the harvest of souls, beyond their capacity to contain. This is the way He thinks about our evangelistic efforts. Expecting anything less is to miss the point of this wonderful story.

But there's something else involved here. Peter's response to the catch is also unique and quite moving. He told Jesus, *"Go away from me, Lord, for I am a sinful man!"* (Luke 5:8 NASB). This is an unusual response to God's goodness revealed in abundance. I know the lesson is about the last days' harvest of souls. But it could only reveal a spiritual reality if it was true as a natural reality first. For example, you'd never compare the joy of the Lord with getting high on drugs. God would never use something that is inherently evil to illustrate something that is good. When Jesus used the abundance of a catch (success in business) to illustrate the harvest of souls that God was anticipating, it first had to work as something legitimate and desirable in business—abundance. What was Peter's business? He caught and sold fish. What was the miracle? Abundant personal provision. Jesus expressed the goodness of a perfect Father to Peter through an abundance of fish that would enable him to provide for his needs and wants plus those of the people who worked for him. The result is astounding. Peter drops to his knees in repentance. This is an important perspective to have in order to fully appreciate the profound nature of Peter's response.

In examining the story, it becomes quite evident that Jesus had not addressed anything about Peter's personal life. Nothing was said about his sinfulness or his need to repent. While I believe strongly in the bold preaching of the Gospel and the need to lead others into true repentance, we have to admit that Jesus accomplished the same results through unusual means. This time He used blessing to lead Peter into a place of right relationship with God the Father. Jesus honored Peter with blessing, and that honor became the "kindness that leads to repentance" that the apostle Paul mentioned in his teaching on salvation (see Rom. 2:4). Our tendency to use the one-size-fits-all approach to sharing the Gospel actually pulls us away from the model Jesus gave us when He did only what He saw the Father do. We can assume that Jesus' unusual approach to Peter was something He saw the Father doing—the Father's heart toward Peter. This process of carrying the Father's heart for people is met with a much higher level of breakthrough in ministry, for the Father sees beyond all that we see and knows what will touch the heart of the person we're serving.

Stories of this nature should amaze us, stirring up a wonder for God as our perfect Father, who sees the uniqueness of every person's heart. Jesus used blessing to bring this man to a place of repentance and full surrender. This is a very uncommon approach to ministry, for many tend to assume that blessing will lead to independence or greed. That is always a possibility. But repentance is also a potential response, as is seen with Peter. The Holy Spirit always knows when to use what tool. It's our responsibility to carry honor in our hearts always, which is easy to do if we discover God's value for people. If we can stop trying to provoke change as though we were Old Testament prophets and instead demonstrate the heart of the good Father, we'll see that transformation of people, cities, and nations for which God Himself longs.

From Old to New

As we discussed in Chapter 8, God withheld rain in the Old Testament because of sin. In the agricultural society of that day, rain represented blessing. Without it, everyone went broke and was left hungry. But in the New Testament, God has a different approach that signifies a change in seasons: *"...love your enemies and pray for those who persecute you, so that you may be sons of your Father who is in heaven; for He causes His sun to rise on the evil and the good, and sends rain on the righteous and the unrighteous"* (Matt. 5:44–45 NASB). He uses blessing to draw people to Himself as a perfect Father who is good. In this passage, Jesus instructs us to adjust our behavior to be just like our Father. And in doing so, we prove or demonstrate that we are His children. Because of His approach to sinners, raining on the just as well as the unjust, we are to correct our behavior to be consistent with His by praying for those who persecute us. This is not to be a prayer of accusation. It is to be "for them" and in the context of our love for them, thus demonstrating who our Father is.

This one principle must be emphasized more, as the evidence of our conversion is seen in our being like our Father, who loves, blesses, and honors people before they are converted. This position makes it more likely that people will discover that God is good.

Seeking an Audience with Jesus

Being with Jesus seemed to be on everyone's mind. Crowds pressed in upon Him until it was difficult to walk down the street of any city He visited. They would sometimes even follow Him into the wilderness, where there was no food or natural supplies for the journey. Either they didn't care or lost all concern for personal needs when they were with Him. There were even times when the crowd would become more aggressive and press in about Him to try to touch His clothing or His body. The demand to be near Him was beyond our understanding. It was much more than what we see today when people are trying to get close to a rock star. And with good reason. Life came from Jesus in a way that marked people forever. And they all wanted that.

Interestingly, not only did the citizens of the communities want to be near Him; even the religious leaders who opposed Him, not believing He was the Messiah, also sought an audience with Him. This is what happened when the woman brought the jar of expensive perfume to anoint Jesus' body before His death and burial (see Luke 7:37). This great story took place in a Pharisee's home.

Jesus wasn't angry with the religious leaders, but He did dislike the fact that often they were the ones who would teach one thing but live another. They were also offended by His putting the needs of people above their interpretation of the Sabbath. It seems that the only people with whom Jesus had consistent problems were these religious leaders. And yet, they sought to be with Him. Even the religious leader named Nicodemus came to Jesus at night because of his desire to be with Him (see John 3:1–3). The point is, everyone wanted to be near Jesus. The ultimate dream would have been to have Jesus come to their home. That's what makes the next story so fascinating.

Honoring the Ultimate Sinner

Once again Jesus is found walking down a crowded street. The people are pressing in about Him to the point that some found it nearly impossible to see or hear what was happening. One such man was a tax collector named Zaccheus. A tax collector in this day was one of the most despised individuals in the community. They were known as thieves. But Zaccheus was not just a tax collector. He was the *chief* tax collector. In other words, he was a thief in charge of other thieves. I suspect that people despised him more than the prostitute or the town drunk. Those kinds of people were easily pitied. But tax collectors stole from them intentionally and unjustly, in the name of being a governmental representative.

As Jesus proceeded through the town, Zaccheus wanted to see what was happening. Because of the size of the crowd as well as his small stature, he simply couldn't see Jesus or what was happening. This is such a beautiful picture: The chief thief wanted to see Jesus. Underneath his greed and self-centeredness was a heart that would respond to God if he were given a chance. It often happens that way. Gold hides in dirt. Jesus saw what others couldn't see because He looked through the eyes of His perfect Father. Zaccheus had enough interest in Jesus to run down the street in the direction that He was walking until he found a tree to climb that enabled him to see what was happening. As Jesus approached, He called him out of the tree, saying, *"Zaccheus, hurry and come down, for today I must stay at your house"* (Luke 19:5 NASB).

This is one of the more familiar stories in the Gospels, although it's found only in Luke. Many of us learned this story in Sunday school, which makes sense—the stories taught to children are often the best ones, as they are the easiest to remember and the principles we need to learn from them are clearly understood. This is certainly true in the story of this tax collector.

Everyone in the crowd wanted to be with Jesus. To have Him come to their house would be the ultimate honor. Yet there are very few times recorded in Scripture where we see Jesus spending time at anyone's home. We know He spent time at Mary, Martha, and Lazarus's home, a wealthy household. He also had a meal or two at the home of a Pharisee, an opponent to His life and message. And now we see Him going to the home of a tax collector, the one many would call the worst sinner in town. Just considering those three examples provides an unusual cross section of the people into whom Jesus longed to pour.

Going to Zaccheus's home created quite a stir. The criticism started immediately, with people questioning Jesus' discernment and spirituality. It's interesting that the thing that kept people from the tax collector was the very thing that drew Jesus to him. He was a sinner, and he knew it. That type of person is in a much better place than a self-righteous person who has insulated himself from an awareness of one's personal need for God. The religious leaders were known for their spiritual blindness, while the prostitute, the tax collectors, and the demonized were aware of their condition. This positioned them to receive help. Awareness of need brings people near to the Kingdom. And each of them had no trouble recognizing Jesus for who He was—the eternal Son of God.

Without preaching a sermon, without any personal rebuke, without casting any shame upon this rich man for his wealth, Jesus led this man into repentance simply by being with him. Honor works wonders. In response to Jesus' kindness, Zaccheus told Him, *"...Half of my possessions I will give to the poor, and if I have defrauded anyone of anything, I will give back four times as much"* (Luke 15:8 NASB). Jesus then responded, *"Today salvation has come to this house, because he, too, is a son of Abraham"* (Luke 15:9 NASB). This beautiful story happened because Jesus, who once again represented the Father well, received Zaccheus before he deserved it. It's what good fathers do. In essence, this tax collector was received before he believed. As a result, he began to move in restitution, which is beautiful evidence of true repentance. It is also notable that Zaccheus was moved with compassion for those in need. None of this was forced. It is the natural byproduct of surrender to Jesus.

THE TEST OF GOD'S GOODNESS

The goodness of God is not a magic wand that we wave over a problem to see it fixed. It is the context in which we do life. Everything we see and experience is defined by that one prevailing reality: God is good. Seeing His goodness is beholding perfect beauty, which in turn becomes the invitation to come to know Him. In such a journey, we automatically celebrate His heart toward us. And while I'm thankful for all the times I've seen an instant answer to the cry of my heart, I'm also grateful for the delays. God is a builder. Sometimes He builds my understanding of Him through breakthroughs and answers, and other times He is building an understanding of His faithfulness in the long haul. This becomes evident through a stability in me that doesn't waver when things look the opposite of how I've prayed. This brings us to two important aspects of our life in Christ: Faith and power. Both are essential spiritual realities for the believer that enable us to demonstrate the goodness of God in both powerful and practical ways. Seeing the role of each enables us to maintain our heart of conviction in the midst of trial.

FAITH

Faith brings breakthrough. Enduring faith brings breakthrough with character. Enduring faith can exist only in the midst of delay and sometimes coincides with confusion or disappointment. And while our answers to the prayer of faith are very important to God, so is the Christ-like character that is formed in us through waiting with trust. Bold faith stands on the shoulders of quiet trust.

The answers we receive reinforce the concept of being a co-laborer with God, who is good. Each answer reveals His nature as a good Father while at the same time enabling us to use the authority given to us as disciples of Jesus to reveal His will on earth. Consider this—that both His nature and His will are seen in answers to prayer. They are vital expressions of God's value for us. Yet in the waiting, we must guard ourselves from creating a theology where unanswered prayers become normal. Losing expectations is how many have protected their hearts from the frustration of delay. Hopelessness is a poor cure for disappointment. Once again, Jesus is the model to follow. As Chris Gore says, "Jesus didn't teach on unanswered prayers because He didn't have any." Brilliantly true. And this is our destiny.

We must learn to "jumpstart" our faith through a change in the exercise of faith. Weightlifters often reach plateaus in their muscle development. One of the tricks they use to ignite muscle growth once they've leveled off is to work that same muscle from a different angle with a different exercise. People often hold God hostage to answer one specific prayer before they move on in life. Many die in that condition, thinking that God failed to answer, when in fact they were stuck and didn't know how to get out of it. Such a focus on *the one area that God needs to answer to prove Himself* works against their personal development. It also works against the area they are targeting in prayer. Such individuals need to step outside of convenience to activate their faith for personal growth. For example, if you pray for people to be healed in your Sunday church gatherings and you're seeing little results, go to the streets to find people in need. Or visit people in the hospitals and/or your own neighbors who are sick. Watch as God uses your exercise of the faith *muscle* from a different angle to develop the faith needed for the issue that concerns you most.

POWER

Power brings breakthrough. Miracles happen often because of the power of God released in and through His people. Wherever we see the power of God displayed, we see transformation and change.

Miracles, signs, and wonders are the fruit of the Holy Spirit's power in the life of the believing believer.

Power is the purpose behind the baptism of the Holy Spirit: *"But you shall receive power..."* (Acts 1:8). Yet the second manifestation of power is equally important. It is the ability to endure until the answer comes. There are two sides to this coin—breakthrough and endurance. It is the exact same concept that we saw with faith. We must develop the lifestyle of endurance without embracing the lack of breakthrough as the norm.

Rolland and Heidi Baker, of Iris Ministries, have been personal friends for close to 20 years now. I don't know of anyone who has seen more miracles in their lives and ministry as they have. Whether it be resurrections of the dead, or blind eyes opened, or the multiplication of food, such displays of God's goodness have become the norm for Iris Ministries. And yet I also don't know of any group who has endured more while waiting for a miracle than they have. This combination of *the effects of Holy Ghost power* is stunning with both breakthrough and endurance.

Instead of creating a theology where lack is normal, it is best to get alone with Jesus and find out why there is no breakthrough. That's what we saw in the story of the disciples and the tormented child in Chapter 10 (see Mark 9:28–29). Regardless of public opinion and well-meaning pastors and theologians who want us to settle for less so as not to be disappointed, holding to the standard set by Jesus to become a generation of extraordinary breakthroughs is vital that we might inherit all that Jesus intended for us.

OUR ULTIMATE CALL

It is in God's heart for His glory to be seen upon the earth. And that glory is seen simultaneously with the discovery of His goodness (see Ex. 33:19). Living in honor, displaying His goodness, provides the setting for nations to come to Christ. This is our ultimate ambition.

If we can hold to the bold preaching of the Gospel while at the same time learning how to live honorably among all peoples, we'll be well positioned to disciple nations. This is the context in which God is seen as good and is ultimately recognized as a good and perfect Father.

ADDENDUM

Psalm 119:68

> You are good and do good; teach me Your statutes.

Genesis 1:31

> God saw all that He had made, and behold, it was very
> good. And there was evening and there was morning, the
> sixth day.

Psalm 104 (the whole chapter)

Psalm 103:8–13

> The Lord is compassionate and gracious, slow to anger
> and abounding in lovingkindness. He will not always
> strive with us, nor will He keep His anger forever. He
> has not dealt with us according to our sins, nor rewarded
> us according to our iniquities. For as high as the heavens
> are above the earth, so great is His lovingkindness toward

those who fear Him. As far as the east is from the west, so far has He removed our transgressions from us. Just as a father has compassion on his children, so the Lord has compassion on those who fear Him.

Zephaniah 3:17

The Lord your God is in your midst, a victorious warrior. He will exult over you with joy, He will be quiet in His love, He will rejoice over you with shouts of joy.

Galatians 5:22–23

But the fruit of the Spirit is love, joy, peace, patience, kindness, goodness, faithfulness, gentleness, self-control; against such things there is no law.

Matthew 7:11

If you then, being evil, know how to give good gifts to your children, how much more will your Father who is in heaven give what is good to those who ask Him!

Exodus 34:5–7

The Lord descended in the cloud and stood there with him as he called upon the name of the Lord. Then the Lord passed by in front of him and proclaimed, "The Lord, the Lord God, compassionate and gracious, slow to anger, and abounding in lovingkindness and truth; who keeps lovingkindness for thousands, who forgives iniquity, transgression and sin; yet He will by no means leave the guilty unpunished, visiting the iniquity of fathers on the children and on the grandchildren to the third and fourth generations.

Acts 14:16–17, NIV

In the past, he let all nations go their own way. Yet he has not left himself without testimony: He has shown kindness by giving you rain from heaven and crops in their seasons; he provides you with plenty of food and fills your hearts with joy.

Acts 17:22–31 (Paul speaking to the men of Athens)

So Paul stood in the midst of the Areopagus and said, "Men of Athens, I observe that you are very religious in all respects. For while I was passing through and examining the objects of your worship, I also found an altar with this inscription, 'TO AN UNKNOWN GOD.' Therefore what you worship in ignorance, this I proclaim to you. The God who made the world and all things in it, since He is Lord of heaven and earth, does not dwell in temples made with hands; nor is He served by human hands, as though He needed anything, since He Himself gives to all people life and breath and all things; and He made from one man every nation of mankind to live on all the face of the earth, having determined their appointed times and the boundaries of their habitation, that they would seek God, if perhaps they might grope for Him and find Him, though He is not far from each one of us; for in Him we live and move and exist, as even some of your own poets have said, 'For we also are His children.' Being then the children of God, we ought not to think that the Divine Nature is like gold or silver or stone, an image formed by the art and thought of man. Therefore having overlooked the times of ignorance, God is now declaring to men that all people everywhere should repent, because He has fixed a day in which He will judge the world in righteousness through a Man whom He has appointed, having furnished proof to all men by raising Him from the dead."

Jesus reveals the love, priorities, and goodness of the Father in His ministry and sacrifice—He is perfect theology.

Hebrews 1:2–3

In these last days God has spoken to us in His Son, whom He appointed heir of all things, through whom also He made the world. And He is the radiance of His glory and the exact representation of His nature, and upholds all things by the word of His power. When He had made purification of sins, He sat down at the right hand of the Majesty on high.

Colossians 1:19

For it was the Father's good pleasure for all the fullness to dwell in Him.

Colossians 2:9

For in Him all the fullness of Deity dwells in bodily form.

John 1:1,18

In the beginning was the Word, and the Word was with God, and the Word was God. ...No one has seen God at any time; the only begotten God who is in the bosom of the Father, He has explained Him.

John 3:16–17

For God so loved the world, that He gave His only begotten Son, that whoever believes in Him shall not perish, but have eternal life. For God did not send the Son into the world to judge the world, but that the world might be saved through Him.

John 14:6–7

Jesus said to him, "I am the way, and the truth, and the life; no one comes to the Father but through Me. If you had known Me, you would have known My Father also; from now on you know Him, and have seen Him."

John 8:1–11,19 (the story of the woman caught in adultery)

But Jesus went to the Mount of Olives. Early in the morning He came again into the temple, and all the people were coming to Him; and He sat down and began to teach them. The scribes and the Pharisees brought a woman caught in adultery, and having set her in the center of the court, they said to Him, "Teacher, this woman has been caught in adultery, in the very act. Now in the Law Moses commanded us to stone such women; what then do You say?" They were saying this, testing Him, so that they might have grounds for accusing Him. But Jesus stooped down and with His finger wrote on the ground. But when they persisted in asking Him, He straightened up, and said to them, "He who is without sin among you, let him be the first to throw a stone at her." Again He stooped down and wrote on the ground. When they heard it, they began to go out one by one, beginning with the older ones, and He was left alone, and the woman, where she was, in the center of the court. Straightening up, Jesus said to her, "Woman, where are they? Did no one condemn you?" She said, "No one, Lord." And Jesus said, "I do not condemn you, either. Go. From now on sin no more."...So they were saying to Him, "Where is Your Father?" Jesus answered, "You know neither Me nor My Father; if you knew Me, you would know My Father also."

God is good regardless of our circumstances.

Nahum 1:7

The Lord is good, a stronghold in the day of trouble, and He knows those who take refuge in Him.

Romans 8:28–32

And we know that God causes all things to work together for good to those who love God, to those who are called according to His purpose. For those whom He foreknew, He also predestined to become conformed to the image of His Son, so that He would be the firstborn among many brethren; and these whom He predestined, He also called; and these whom He called, He also justified; and these whom He justified, He also glorified. What then shall we say to these things? If God is for us, who is against us? He who did not spare His own Son, but delivered Him over for us all, how will He not also with Him freely give us all things?

James 1:17

Every good thing given and every perfect gift is from above, coming down from the Father of lights, with whom there is no variation or shifting shadow.

Acts 16:23–26 (Paul and Silas in prison)

When they had struck them with many blows, they threw them into prison, commanding the jailer to guard them securely; and he, having received such a command, threw them into the inner prison and fastened their feet in the stocks. But about midnight Paul and Silas were praying and singing hymns of praise to God, and the prisoners were listening to them; and suddenly there came a great earthquake, so that the foundations of the prison house were shaken; and immediately all the doors were opened and everyone's chains were unfastened.

Enemies come to steal and kill, but Jesus came to destroy demonic works and to give us abundant life.

John 10:10–11

The thief comes only to steal and kill and destroy; I came that they may have life, and have it abundantly. I am

*the good shepherd; the good shepherd lays down His life
for the sheep.*

1 John 3:8

*The one who practices sin is of the devil; for the devil has
sinned from the beginning. The Son of God appeared for
this purpose, to destroy the works of the devil.*

1 Peter 5:8–10, NIV

*Be alert and of sober mind. Your enemy the devil prowls
around like a roaring lion looking for someone to devour.
Resist him, standing firm in the faith, because you know
that the family of believers throughout the world is
undergoing the same kind of sufferings. And the God of
all grace, who called you to his eternal glory in Christ,
after you have suffered a little while, will himself restore
you and make you strong, firm and steadfast.*

Ephesians 6:12, NIV

*For our struggle is not against flesh and blood, but
against the rulers, against the authorities, against the
powers of this dark world and against the spiritual forces
of evil in the heavenly realms.*

Matthew 9:11–13

*When the Pharisees saw this, they said to His disciples,
"Why is your Teacher eating with the tax collectors and
sinners?" But when Jesus heard this, He said, "It is not
those who are healthy who need a physician, but those*

who are sick. But go and learn what this means: 'I desire compassion, and not sacrifice,' for I did not come to call the righteous, but sinners."

Mark 5:1–19 (the Garasene demoniac)

They came to the other side of the sea, into the country of the Gerasenes. When He got out of the boat, immediately a man from the tombs with an unclean spirit met Him, and he had his dwelling among the tombs. And no one was able to bind him anymore, even with a chain; because he had often been bound with shackles and chains, and the chains had been torn apart by him and the shackles broken in pieces, and no one was strong enough to subdue him. Constantly, night and day, he was screaming among the tombs and in the mountains, and gashing himself with stones. Seeing Jesus from a distance, he ran up and bowed down before Him; and shouting with a loud voice, he said, "What business do we have with each other, Jesus, Son of the Most High God? I implore You by God, do not torment me!" For He had been saying to him, "Come out of the man, you unclean spirit!" And He was asking him, "What is your name?" And he said to Him, "My name is Legion; for we are many." And he began to implore Him earnestly not to send them out of the country. Now there was a large herd of swine feeding nearby on the mountain. The demons implored him, saying, "Send us into the swine so that we may enter them." Jesus gave them permission. And coming out, the unclean spirits entered the swine; and the herd rushed down the steep bank into the sea, about two thousand of them; and they were drowned in the sea. Their herdsmen ran away and reported it in the city and in the country. And the people came to see what it was that had happened. They came to Jesus and observed the man who had been demon-possessed sitting down, clothed and in his right mind, the very man who had had the "legion"; and they became frightened. Those who had seen it described to them how it had happened to the demon-possessed man, and all about the swine. And they began to implore Him to leave their region. As He was getting into the boat, the man who had been demon-possessed was imploring Him that he might accompany Him. And He did not let him, but He said to him, "Go home to your people and report to them what great things the Lord has done for you, and how He had mercy on you."

God is generous. As we remember and retell what He has done through testimonies, He's able and eager to do it again.

John 3:16

For God so loved the world, that He gave His only begotten Son, that whoever believes in Him shall not perish, but have eternal life.

Revelation 12:11

And they overcame him because of the blood of the Lamb and because of the word of their testimony, and they did not love their life even when faced with death.

Revelation 19:10

Then I fell at his feet to worship him. But he said to me, "Do not do that; I am a fellow servant of yours and your brethren who hold the testimony of Jesus; worship God. For the testimony of Jesus is the spirit of prophecy."

Joshua 4:1–9 (the story of the twelve memorial stones of testimony)

Now when all the nation had finished crossing the Jordan, the Lord spoke to Joshua, saying, "Take for yourselves twelve men from the people, one man from each tribe, and command them, saying, 'Take up for yourselves twelve stones from here out of the middle of the Jordan, from the place where the priests' feet are standing firm, and carry them over with you and lay them down in the lodging place where you will lodge tonight.'" So Joshua called the twelve men whom he had appointed from the sons of Israel, one man from each tribe; and Joshua said to them, "Cross again to the ark of the Lord your God into the middle of the Jordan, and each of you take up a stone on his shoulder, according to the number of the tribes of the sons of Israel. Let this be a sign among you, so that when your children ask later, saying, 'What do these stones mean to you?' then you shall say to them, 'Because the waters of the Jordan were cut off before the ark of the covenant of the Lord; when it crossed the Jordan, the waters of the Jordan were cut off.' So these stones shall become a memorial to the sons of Israel forever." Thus the sons of Israel did as Joshua commanded, and took up twelve stones from the middle of the Jordan, just as the Lord spoke to Joshua, according to the number of the tribes of the sons of Israel; and they carried them over with them to the lodging place and put them down there. Then Joshua set up twelve stones in the middle of the Jordan at the place where the feet of the priests who carried the ark of the covenant were standing, and they are there to this day.

GOD IS GOOD—WHAT DOES THIS MEAN?

God is for us. He chose to redeem us from our sin.

Romans 5:8

But God demonstrates His own love toward us, in that while we were yet sinners, Christ died for us.

Romans 8:30–32

And these whom He predestined, He also called; and these whom He called, He also justified; and these whom He justified, He also glorified. What then shall we say to these things? If God is for us, who is against us? He who did not spare His own Son, but delivered Him over for us all, how will He not also with Him freely give us all things?

2 Corinthians 5:19

Namely, that God was in Christ reconciling the world to Himself, not counting their trespasses against them, and He has committed to us the word of reconciliation.

God is not mad at us.

2 Peter 3:9, NIV

The Lord is not slow in keeping his promise, as some understand slowness. Instead he is patient with you, not wanting anyone to perish, but everyone to come to repentance.

1 Thessalonians 5:9, NIV

For God did not appoint us to suffer wrath but to receive salvation through our Lord Jesus Christ.

Romans 14:17–18

For the kingdom of God is not eating and drinking, but righteousness and peace and joy in the Holy Spirit. For he who in this way serves Christ is acceptable to God and approved by men.

John 10:10

The thief comes only to steal and kill and destroy; I came that they may have life, and have it abundantly.

Romans 2:4, NIV

Or do you show contempt for the riches of his kindness, forbearance and patience, not realizing that God's kindness is intended to lead you to repentance?

Zephaniah 3:17

The Lord your God is in your midst, a victorious warrior. He will exult over you with joy, He will be quiet in His love, He will rejoice over you with shouts of joy.

God's desire is to prosper us in every area of our lives: physically, mentally, spiritually, emotionally, and vocationally.

Psalm 103:1–5, NIV

Praise the Lord, my soul...and forget not all his bene-fits—who forgives all your sins and heals all your diseases, who redeems your life from the pit and crowns you with love and compassion, who satisfies your desires with good things so that your youth is renewed like the eagle's.

2 Corinthians 9:8–10

And God is able to make all grace abound to you, so that always having all sufficiency in everything, you may have an abundance for every good deed; as it is written, "He scattered abroad, He gave to the poor, His righteousness endures forever." Now He who supplies seed to the sower and bread for food will supply and multiply your seed for sowing and increase the harvest of your righteousness.

Genesis 12:1–3

Now the Lord said to Abram, "Go forth from your country, and from your relatives and from your father's house, to the land which I will show you; and I will make you a great nation, and I will bless you, and make your name great; and so you shall be a blessing; and I will bless those who bless you, and the one who curses you I will curse. And in you all the families of the earth will be blessed."

Isaiah 26:3

The steadfast of mind You will keep in perfect peace, because he trusts in You.

Isaiah 53:4–6

Surely our griefs He Himself bore, and our sorrows He carried; yet we ourselves esteemed Him stricken, smitten of God, and afflicted. But He was pierced through for our transgressions, He was crushed for our iniquities; the chastening for our well-being fell upon Him, and by His scourging we are healed. All of us like sheep have gone astray, each of us has turned to his own way; but the Lord has caused the iniquity of us all to fall on Him.

Luke 9:6,56

Departing, they began going throughout the villages, preaching the gospel and healing everywhere..."for the Son of Man did not come to destroy men's lives, but to save them." And they went on to another village.

3 John 1:2

Beloved, I pray that in all respects you may prosper and be in good health, just as your soul prospers.

Jeremiah 29:11

"For I know the plans that I have for you,'" declares the Lord, "'plans for welfare and not for calamity to give you a future and a hope."

God does not cause sickness to teach people lessons or to punish them. Jesus is our New Covenant model, as He healed all the sick people He encountered.

Matthew 4:23

Jesus was going throughout all Galilee, teaching in their synagogues and proclaiming the gospel of the kingdom, and healing every kind of disease and every kind of sickness among the people.

Matthew 8:2–3

And a leper came to Him and bowed down before Him, and said, "Lord, if You are willing, You can make me clean." Jesus stretched out His hand and touched him, saying, "I am willing; be cleansed." And immediately his leprosy was cleansed.

Acts 10:38

You know of Jesus of Nazareth, how God anointed Him with the Holy Spirit and with power, and how He went about doing good and healing all who were oppressed by the devil, for God was with Him.

> **We live from the premise that God
> wants to save and heal everyone.**

1 Timothy 2:4 NIV

...who wants all people to be saved and to come to a knowledge of the truth.

Acts 10:38

You know of Jesus of Nazareth, how God anointed Him with the Holy Spirit and with power, and how He went about doing good and healing all who were oppressed by the devil, for God was with Him.

Ezekiel 33:11

Say to them, "As I live!" declares the Lord God, "I take no pleasure in the death of the wicked, but rather that the wicked turn from his way and live. Turn back, turn back from your evil ways! Why then will you die, O house of Israel?"

Matthew 4:23–24

Jesus was going throughout all Galilee, teaching in their synagogues and proclaiming the gospel of the kingdom, and healing every kind of disease and every kind of sickness among the people. The news about Him spread throughout all Syria; and they brought to Him all who were ill, those suffering with various diseases and pains, demoniacs, epileptics, paralytics; and He healed them.

Matthew 8:1–3

When Jesus came down from the mountain, large crowds followed Him. And a leper came to Him and bowed down before Him, and said, "Lord, if You are willing, You can make me clean." Jesus stretched out His hand and touched him, saying, "I am willing; be cleansed." And immediately his leprosy was cleansed.

Matthew 8:16–17

When evening came, they brought to Him many who were demon-possessed; and He cast out the spirits with a word, and healed all who were ill. This was to fulfill what was spoken through Isaiah the prophet: "He Himself took our infirmities and carried away our diseases."

Matthew 9:35

Jesus was going through all the cities and villages, teaching in their synagogues and proclaiming the gospel of the kingdom, and healing every kind of disease and every kind of sickness.

Matthew 14:34–36

When they had crossed over, they came to land at Gennesaret. And when the men of that place recognized Him, they sent word into all that surrounding district and brought to Him all who were sick; and they implored Him that they might just touch the fringe of His cloak; and as many as touched it were cured.

Mark 6:56

Wherever He entered villages, or cities, or countryside, they were laying the sick in the market places, and imploring Him that they might just touch the fringe of His cloak; and as many as touched it were being cured.

Luke 9:11

But the crowds were aware of this and followed Him; and welcoming them, He began speaking to them about the kingdom of God and curing those who had need of healing.

God will never take His plans or His gifts from our life.

Romans 11:29

For the gifts and the calling of God are irrevocable.

Romans 8:28

And we know that God causes all things to work together for good to those who love God, to those who are called according to His purpose.

Ephesians 1:4–6

Just as He chose us in Him before the foundation of the world, that we would be holy and blameless before Him. In love He predestined us to adoption as sons through Jesus Christ to Himself, according to the kind intention of His will, to the praise of the glory of His grace, which He freely bestowed on us in the Beloved.

> **God sees us as masterpieces. His process and pruning are always meant to reveal our true identity and release us into fullness of life.**

Ephesians 2:10

For we are His workmanship, created in Christ Jesus for good works, which God prepared beforehand so that we would walk in them.

Psalm 139:13–17

For You formed my inward parts; You wove me in my mother's womb. I will give thanks to You, for I am fearfully and wonderfully made; wonderful are Your works, and my soul knows it very well. My frame was not hidden from You, when I was made in secret, and skillfully wrought in the depths of the earth; Your eyes have seen my unformed substance; and in Your book were all written the days that were ordained for me, when as yet there was not one of them. How precious also are Your thoughts to me, O God! How vast is the sum of them!

John 15:1–2

I am the true vine, and My Father is the vinedresser. Every branch in Me that does not bear fruit, He takes away; and every branch that bears fruit, He prunes it so that it may bear more fruit.

Hebrews 12:5–13

And you have forgotten the exhortation which is addressed to you as sons, "My son, do not regard lightly the discipline of the Lord, nor faint when you are reproved by Him; for those whom the Lord loves He disciplines, and He scourges every son whom He receives." It is for discipline that you endure; God deals with you as with sons; for what son is there whom his father does not discipline? But if you are without discipline, of which all have become partakers, then you are illegitimate children and not sons. Furthermore, we had earthly fathers to discipline us, and we respected them; shall we not much rather be subject to the Father of spirits, and live? For they disciplined us for a short time as seemed best to them, but He disciplines us for our good, so that we may share His holiness. All discipline for the moment seems not to be joyful, but sorrowful; yet to those who have been trained by it, afterwards it yields the peaceful fruit of righteousness. Therefore, strengthen the hands that are weak and the knees that are feeble, and make straight paths for your feet, so that the limb which is lame may not be put out of joint, but rather be healed.

God personally hears and always responds to our prayers.

1 John 5:14–15

This is the confidence which we have before Him, that, if we ask anything according to His will, He hears us. And if we know that He hears us in whatever we ask, we know that we have the requests which we have asked from Him.

James 1:5,17

But if any of you lacks wisdom, let him ask of God, who gives to all generously and without reproach, and it will be given to him. …Every good thing given and every perfect gift is from above, coming down from the Father of lights, with whom there is no variation or shifting shadow.

Romans 8:26–27,32

In the same way the Spirit also helps our weakness; for we do not know how to pray as we should, but the Spirit Himself intercedes for us with groanings too deep for words; and He who searches the hearts knows what the mind of the Spirit is, because He intercedes for the saints according to the will of God. …He who did not spare His own Son, but delivered Him over for us all, how will He not also with Him freely give us all things?

Matthew 7:7

Ask, and it will be given to you; seek, and you will find; knock, and it will be opened to you.

Luke 18:1–8 (the parable of the unrighteous judge)

Now He was telling them a parable to show that at all times they ought to pray and not to lose heart, saying, "In a certain city there was a judge who did not fear

God and did not respect man. There was a widow in that city, and she kept coming to him, saying, 'Give me legal protection from my opponent.' For a while he was unwilling; but afterward he said to himself, 'Even though I do not fear God nor respect man, yet because this widow bothers me, I will give her legal protection, otherwise by continually coming she will wear me out.'" And the Lord said, "Hear what the unrighteous judge said; now, will not God bring about justice for His elect who cry to Him day and night, and will He delay long over them? I tell you that He will bring about justice for them quickly. However, when the Son of Man comes, will He find faith on the earth?"

2 Corinthians 1:20

For as many as are the promises of God, in Him they are yes; therefore also through Him is our Amen to the glory of God through us.

GOD IS GOOD—DON'T MISUNDERSTAND...

We can't do whatever we want and expect God to always bless us. God remains the ultimate Judge of every human being.

1 John 1:5–7

This is the message we have heard from Him and announce to you, that God is Light, and in Him there is no darkness at all. If we say that we have fellowship with Him and yet walk in the darkness, we lie and do not practice the truth; but if we walk in the Light as He Himself is in the Light, we have fellowship with one another, and the blood of Jesus His Son cleanses us from all sin.

Hebrews 10:26–27

For if we go on sinning willfully after receiving the knowledge of the truth, there no longer remains a sacrifice for sins, but a terrifying expectation of judgment and the fury of a fire which will consume the adversaries.

2 Timothy 2:19, NIV

Nevertheless, God's solid foundation stands firm, sealed with this inscription: "The Lord knows those who are his," and, "Everyone who confesses the name of the Lord must turn away from wickedness."

Proverbs 8:13

The fear of the Lord is to hate evil; pride and arrogance and the evil way and the perverted mouth, I hate.

Hebrews 9:27

And inasmuch as it is appointed for men to die once and after this comes judgment.

2 Corinthians 5:10

For we must all appear before the judgment seat of Christ, so that each one may be recompensed for his deeds in the body, according to what he has done, whether good or bad.

Galatians 5:13–24

For you were called to freedom, brethren; only do not turn your freedom into an opportunity for the flesh, but through love serve one another. For the whole Law is fulfilled in one word, in the statement, "You shall love your neighbor as yourself." But if you bite and devour one another, take care that you are not consumed by one another. But I say, walk by the Spirit, and you will not carry out the desire of the flesh. For the flesh sets its desire against the Spirit, and the Spirit against the flesh; for these are in opposition to one another, so that you may not do the things that you please. But if you are led by the Spirit, you are not under the Law. Now the deeds of the flesh are evident, which are: immorality, impurity, sensuality, idolatry, sorcery, enmities, strife, jealousy, outbursts of anger, disputes, dissensions, factions, envying, drunkenness, carousing, and things like these, of which I forewarn you, just as I have forewarned you, that those who practice such things will not inherit the kingdom of God. But the fruit of the Spirit is love, joy, peace, patience, kindness, goodness, faithfulness, gentleness, self-control; against such things there is no law. Now those who belong to Christ Jesus have crucified the flesh with its passions and desires.

God is hurt by our sinful actions and will lovingly confront us if and when we sin.

Ephesians 4:17–32

So this I say, and affirm together with the Lord, that you walk no longer just as the Gentiles also walk, in the futility of their mind, being darkened in their understanding, excluded from the life of God because of the ignorance that is in them, because of the hardness of their heart; and they, having become callous, have given themselves over to sensuality for the practice of every kind of impurity with greediness. But you did not learn Christ in this way, if indeed you have heard Him and have been taught in Him, just as truth is in Jesus, that, in reference to your former manner of life, you lay aside the old self, which is being corrupted in accordance with the lusts of deceit, and that you be renewed in the spirit of your mind, and put on the new self, which in the likeness of God has been created in righteousness and holiness of the truth. Therefore, laying aside falsehood, speak truth each one of you with his neighbor, for we are members one of another. Be angry, and yet do not sin; do not let the sun go down on your anger, and do not give the devil an opportunity. He who steals must steal no longer; but rather he must labor, performing with his own hands what is good, so that he will have something to share with one who has need. Let no unwholesome word proceed from your mouth, but only such a word as is good for edification according to the need of the moment, so that it will give grace to those who hear. Do not grieve the Holy Spirit of

God, by whom you were sealed for the day of redemption. Let all bitterness and wrath and anger and clamor and slander be put away from you, along with all malice. Be kind to one another, tender-hearted, forgiving each other, just as God in Christ also has forgiven you.

John 15:2

Every branch in Me that does not bear fruit, He takes away; and every branch that bears fruit, He prunes it so that it may bear more fruit.

Despite God's goodness and love, some people will still choose hell over Heaven.

John 3:17–18

For God did not send the Son into the world to judge the world, but that the world might be saved through Him. He who believes in Him is not judged; he who does not believe has been judged already, because he has not believed in the name of the only begotten Son of God.

Romans 1:20–23

For since the creation of the world His invisible attributes, His eternal power and divine nature, have been clearly seen, being understood through what has been made, so that they are without excuse. For even though they knew God, they did not honor Him as God or give thanks, but they became futile in their speculations, and their foolish heart was darkened. Professing to be wise, they became fools, and exchanged the glory of the incorruptible God

*for an image in the form of corruptible man and of birds
and four-footed animals and crawling creatures.*

Romans 8:1–8

*Therefore there is now no condemnation for those who
are in Christ Jesus. For the law of the Spirit of life in
Christ Jesus has set you free from the law of sin and
of death. For what the Law could not do, weak as it
was through the flesh, God did: sending His own Son
in the likeness of sinful flesh and as an offering for sin,
He condemned sin in the flesh, so that the requirement
of the Law might be fulfilled in us, who do not walk
according to the flesh but according to the Spirit. For
those who are according to the flesh set their minds on
the things of the flesh, but those who are according to the
Spirit, the things of the Spirit. For the mind set on the
flesh is death, but the mind set on the Spirit is life and
peace, because the mind set on the flesh is hostile toward
God; for it does not subject itself to the law of God, for it
is not even able to do so, and those who are in the flesh
cannot please God.*

Matthew 7:21–23

*Not everyone who says to Me, "Lord, Lord," will enter
the kingdom of heaven, but he who does the will of My
Father who is in heaven will enter. Many will say to Me
on that day, "Lord, Lord, did we not prophesy in Your
name, and in Your name cast out demons, and in Your
name perform many miracles?" And then I will declare*

to them, "I never knew you; depart from Me, you who practice lawlessness."

The life of a believer is not free from trials or persecution.

2 Timothy 3:12

Indeed, all who desire to live godly in Christ Jesus will be persecuted.

John 16:33

These things I have spoken to you, so that in Me you may have peace. In the world you have tribulation, but take courage; I have overcome the world.

Romans 8:31–39

What then shall we say to these things? If God is for us, who is against us? He who did not spare His own Son, but delivered Him over for us all, how will He not also with Him freely give us all things? Who will bring a charge against God's elect? God is the one who justifies; who is the one who condemns? Christ Jesus is He who died, yes, rather who was raised, who is at the right hand of God, who also intercedes for us. Who will separate us from the love of Christ? Will tribulation, or distress, or persecution, or famine, or nakedness, or peril, or sword? Just as it is written, "For Your sake we are being put to death all day long; we were considered as sheep to be slaughtered." But in all these things we overwhelmingly conquer through Him who loved us. For I am convinced that neither death, nor life, nor angels, nor principalities, *nor things present, nor things to come, nor powers, nor height, nor depth, nor any other created thing, will be able to separate us from the love of God, which is in Christ Jesus our Lord.*

Philippians 3:10

That I may know Him and the power of His resurrection and the fellowship of His sufferings, being conformed to His death.

Psalm 34:19

Many are the afflictions of the righteous, but the Lord delivers him out of them all.

James 1:2–4

Consider it all joy, my brethren, when you encounter various trials, knowing that the testing of your faith produces endurance. And let endurance have its perfect result, so that you may be perfect and complete, lacking in nothing.

Every believer is responsible to steward and grow the gifts and talents God has given us.

Matthew 25:14–30 (the parable of the talents)

For it is just like a man about to go on a journey, who called his own slaves and entrusted his possessions to them. To one he gave five talents, to another, two, and to another, one, each according to his own ability; and he went on his journey. Immediately the one who had received the five talents went and traded with them, and gained five more talents. In the same manner the one who had received the two talents gained two more. But he who received the one talent went away, and dug a hole in the ground and hid his master's money. Now after a long time the master of those slaves came and settled accounts with them. The one who had received the five talents came up and brought five more talents, saying, "Master, you entrusted five talents to me. See, I have gained five more talents." His master said to him, "Well done, good and faithful slave. You were faithful with a few things, I will put you in charge of many things; enter into the joy of your master." Also the one who had received the two talents came up and said, "Master, you entrusted two talents to me. See, I have gained two more talents." His master said to him, "Well done, good and faithful slave. You were faithful with a few things, I will put you in charge of many things; enter into the joy of your master." And the one also who had received the one talent came up and said, "Master, I knew you to be a hard man, reaping where you did not sow and gathering where you scattered no seed. And I was afraid, and went away and hid your talent in the ground. See, you have what is yours." But his master answered and said to him, "You wicked, lazy slave, you knew that I reap where I did not sow and gather where I scattered no seed. Then you ought to have put my money in the bank, and on my arrival I would have received my money back with interest. Therefore take away the talent from him, and give it to the one who has the ten talents." For to everyone who has, more shall be given, and he will have an abundance; but from the one who does not have, even what he does have shall be taken away. Throw out the worthless slave into the outer darkness; in that place there will be weeping and gnashing of teeth.

2 Timothy 1:6

For this reason I remind you to kindle afresh the gift of God which is in you through the laying on of my hands.

1 Corinthians 9:24–27

Do you not know that those who run in a race all run, but only one receives the prize? Run in such a way that you may win. Everyone who competes in the games exercises self-control in all things. They then do it to receive a perishable wreath, but we an imperishable. Therefore I run in such a way, as not without aim; I box in such a way, as not beating the air; but I discipline my body and make it my slave, so that, after I have preached to others, I myself will not be disqualified.

Philippians 3:12–14

Not that I have already obtained it or have already become perfect, but I press on so that I may lay hold of that for which also I was laid hold of by Christ Jesus. Brethren, I do not regard myself as having laid hold of it yet; but one thing I do: forgetting what lies behind and reaching forward to what lies ahead, I press on toward the goal for the prize of the upward call of God in Christ Jesus.

In His goodness, God doesn't always respond to our prayers in the way or timing we expect.

2 Peter 3:9

The Lord is not slow about His promise, as some count slowness, but is patient toward you, not wishing for any to perish but for all to come to repentance.

Isaiah 55:8–9

"For My thoughts are not your thoughts, nor are your ways My ways," declares the Lord. "For as the heavens are higher than the earth, so are My ways higher than your ways, and My thoughts than your thoughts."

Luke 18:1–8 (the parable of the unrighteous judge)

Now He was telling them a parable to show that at all times they ought to pray and not to lose heart, saying, "In a certain city there was a judge who did not fear God and did not respect man. There was a widow in that city, and she kept coming to him, saying, 'Give me legal protection from my opponent.' For a while he was unwilling; but afterward he said to himself, 'Even though I do not fear God nor respect man, yet because this widow bothers me, I will give her legal protection, otherwise by continually coming she will wear me out.'" And the Lord said, "Hear what the unrighteous judge said; now, will not God bring about justice for His elect who cry to Him day and night, and will He delay long over them? I tell you that He will bring about justice for them quickly. However, when the Son of Man comes, will He find faith on the earth?"

Philippians 4:6–7

Be anxious for nothing, but in everything by prayer and supplication with thanksgiving let your requests be made known to God. And the peace of God, which surpasses all comprehension, will guard your hearts and minds in Christ Jesus.

ABOUT BILL JOHNSON

Bill Johnson is a fifth-generation pastor with a rich heritage in the Holy Spirit. Bill and his wife, Beni, are the senior leaders of Bethel Church in Redding, California, and serve a growing number of churches that cross denominational lines, demonstrate power, and partner for revival. Bill's vision is for all believers to experience God's presence and operate in the miraculous—as expressed in his bestselling books *When Heaven Invades Earth* and *Hosting the Presence*. The Johnsons have three children and nine grandchildren.

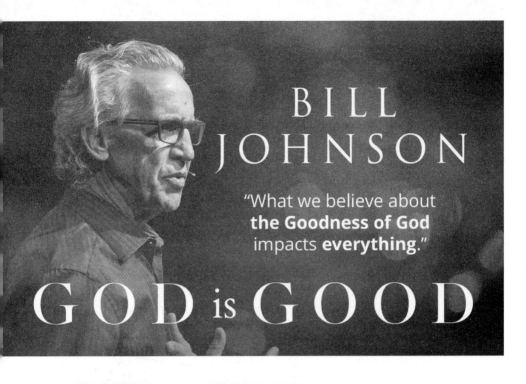

BILL JOHNSON

"What we believe about **the Goodness of God** impacts **everything**."

GOD is GOOD

God is Good
He's Better Than You Think
Bill Johnson
$21.99

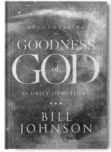

Encountering the
Goodness of God
90 Daily Devotions
Bill Johnson
$15.99

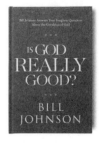

Is God Really Good?
Bill Johnson Answers Your
Toughest Questions About
the Goodness of God
Bill Johnson
$14.99

God is Good
Video Curriculum
Bill Johnson
$99.99

God is Really Good
Children's Book
Bill Johnson, Seth Dahl
$16.99

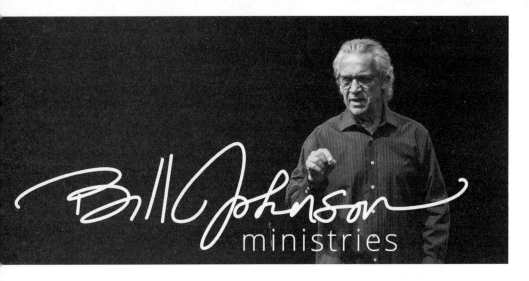

Bill Johnson ministries

BILL JOHNSON is a fifth-generation pastor with a rich heritage in the movement and works of the Holy Spirit. Bill and his wife, Beni, who are senior leaders of Bethel Church in Redding, California, also serve a growing number of churches that cross denominational lines, exhibit power, and partner together for revival.

The vision of Bill Johnson Ministries is to equip Christ-followers to become Heaven's transformational representatives on Earth - equipping people in all spheres of influence to experience God's presence and operate in His Kingdom power. Bill is also the bestselling author of many books, including *When Heaven Invades Earth*, *Hosting the Presence*, *Supernatural Power of a Transformed Mind* and co-author of *Essential Guide to Healing* with Randy Clark. The Johnsons have three children and nine grandchildren.

OTHER RESOURCES FROM BILL JOHNSON

 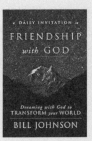 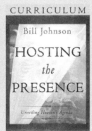  

| BOOKS | DEVOTIONALS | TEACHING CURRICULUM & BIBLE STUDIES | CD, DVD, & DIGITAL AUDIO AND VIDEO | MP3 COLLECTIONS |

CONNECT WITH PASTOR BILL JOHNSON

website: bjm.org • **media:** Bethel.tv • **resources:** shop.ibethel.org
facebook: facebook.com/BillJohnsonMinistries

BILL JOHNSON
GOD is GOOD
VIDEO CURRICULUM

Available everywhere books are sold.

Full Curriculum Set • $99.99
978-0-7684-1034-1

- **Interactive Manual** • $19.99
978-0-7684-1036-5

- **Leader's Guide** • $14.99
978-0-7684-1037-2

- **DVD Study** • $59.99
978-0-7684-1035-8

Also available as an **e-course** through **Bethel.tv**

Ideal for small groups, church classes and personal study, *God is Good* curriculum features **8 dynamic DVD sessions recorded live at Bethel Church** and 8 weeks of powerful interactive discipleship training.

Learn how to:

- **clearly discern** the difference between the will of God and the enemy's plans.
- **confidently pray** for breakthrough, believe for miracles, and have faith for God to move.
- **find rest** in God's unchanging character, even when prayers aren't immediately answered.
- **discover God's goodness** in both the Old and New Testaments.
- **encounter Jesus Christ** as perfect revelation of a good Father.
- **partner with God** to release supernatural solutions to a world in chaos.

Build your life on the solid foundation of God's goodness! Bring Heaven to Earth and change the atmosphere around you!